A Journey
of Spiritual Awakening

A Journey of Spiritual Awakening

HARNESSING YOUR INTUITIVE GIFTS

Judy Brown
with Robyn Burnett

ECW PRESS

Published by ECW PRESS
2120 Queen Street East, Suite 200, Toronto, Ontario, Canada M4E 1E2

NATIONAL LIBRARY OF CANADA CATALOGUING IN PUBLICATION

Brown, Judy
A journey of spiritual awakening: harnessing your intuitive
gifts / Judy Brown; with Robyn Burnett.

ISBN 1-55022-591-X

1. Psychic ability. 2. New Age movement. I. Burnett, Robyn (Robyn S.) II. Title.

BF1031.B76 2003   133.8   C2003-902183-1

Editor: Tracey Millen
Cover and Text Design: Tania Craan
Cover Image: David W. Hamilton/Getty Images
Production and Typesetting: Mary Bowness
Printing: Gauvin Press

This book is set in Julia and Minion

The publication of *A Journey of Spiritual Awakening* has been generously supported by the
Canada Council, the Ontario Arts Council, and the Government of Canada through the
Book Publishing Industry Development Program. Canada

DISTRIBUTION
CANADA: Jaguar Book Group, 100 Armstrong Avenue, Georgetown, ON, L7G 5S4

UNITED STATES: Independent Publishers Group, 814 North Franklin Street,
Chicago, Illinois 60610

PRINTED AND BOUND IN CANADA

ECW PRESS
ecwpress.com

To all my relations, especially the youth of today

Table of Contents

Acknowledgements

It is very important for me to acknowledge the teachers and healers, past and present, that have walked into my life.

Grandfather William Commanda, keeper of sacred belts: The Jay Treaty Belt, The Seven Fires Prophecy Belt, and The Peace Treaty Belt of 1701. I'd like to honor him for his teachings, and for sharing his time and his home for all who come for enlightenment and healing in Maniwaki, Quebec.

Grandmother Jeorgina Larocque for sharing her wisdom with me, and her husband, Bert, for welcoming me into his fold, the White Buffalo Clan, Micmac nation. For this I am deeply honored.

Grayhawk, whose storytelling has lightened my heart and guided me in my personal growth, and his wife, Linda, who with loving arms invited me to share their home, and whose nurturing and caring has blessed my heart.

Brenda Grey, whose counseling helped heal my heart and helped me regain my spirit. And her husband, Rob, whose talents are too many to mention and who gifted me with a picture that he painted, which I titled "The Forest of the Mist" and has given me opportunity to drift into a world of peace, tranquility, and insight.

Great thanks to my special friends, Cathryn and Evan

Evans, whose friendship has honored all that I am.

Sequoya Trueblood for teaching me wisdom and giving me opportunity to soar in spirit.

To ECW Press, who dared to venture onto paths unknown with me. Hugs. What else can I say? To Sanjay, whose energy served to give me a push when I needed it. Thank you. And to my writer mentor, Robyn. My dear ethereal sister, thank you again for being here in light and love, and sharing your many talents with me.

To all my family, who, without them, I would not have learnt the lessons I needed and gathered the wisdom that I have. For this, I honor you.

For all of those, too many to mention, who have lived and laughed with me in a small way, or a big way, thank you.

For all my clients, who have shared a moment in time with me, who perhaps I have helped in some small way, and in a great way, your journeys have only enhanced my learning.

And most of all, for all those who have yet to come, whose paths will intertwine with mine, I give great thanks for the lessons and the wisdom that you will give me.

Introduction

When I was five or six years of age, lying in bed in the middle of the night, I suddenly awakened and saw this big ball of light coming forward from the doorway. Initially the size of a beach ball, it became larger and larger as it approached me. Terrified at first, I kept shaking my older sister, who shared the double bed with me. I tried to wake her, but she remained asleep. I couldn't even yell for my mom or my dad; I was too afraid. And this ball of light kept floating closer and closer . . .

Then, I could see little baby lambs coming out from the ball of light. My fear turned to fascination. In the middle of these little lambs was a normal-sized boy about my age with dirty blond curly hair, just below his ears. His right leg was withered and rested in a wooden wheelbarrow, which he pushed along. He was wearing a short sleeved T-shirt with large colored stripes and knee-high pants, revealing the withered leg. More baby sheep were following him. They all came up on the bed and we had a conversation.

I can remember being overcome with exceptional joy and feeling no fear. While I cannot remember the exact words he used, I sensed that everything was going to be okay and I would never be alone. He reassured me again that he would always be around, then the sheep left and he followed, and as he did, the light faded. Once he was gone, I went back to sleep. Through the years, I kept what transpired that night to myself, but I can still see it to this day. This was my earliest memory of connecting with the ethereal world.

This book was not written with any intent to change anyone's views, opinions, or thoughts. It was written with the intent of offering assistance in learning to love and honor all that you are — past, present, and future — by sharing my own journey. The greatest testimonial and success story that I can give is my own. I choose to use my personal experiences so you can recognize that I have indeed had to overcome major obstacles to get where I am today. I am no different from anyone else in that respect. The stories told are from my perspective and memories, and certainly have not been written with any sort of malice, judgment, or contempt when it comes to anyone else involved in this story. They are all steps in the process of my growth and learning. They help to speak of how my gifts flowed in and out of my life over the years. If it weren't for these lessons, I wouldn't have grown. Even if the others around me didn't know they gave me those gifts, they *gave me those gifts*. So, today I have nothing but thanks for all the shared journeys I have taken. That, however, doesn't mean I *liked* what I went through, or that I *have* to like what I subjected myself too. It does mean that with this acknowledgement, with this learning, you can benefit from my lessons if you choose. If any of the roads you've walked are even similar to anything I've traveled, I pray you can see the gifts in your journeys rather than the anger, the bitterness, the fear, and the hatred. Should this book help one person in this vast world of ours, I have accomplished what I set out to do.

SESSION ONE

Welcome

Before I begin a session with a client, I prepare the room. There are wind chimes in each of the four corners: north, south, east, west. I ring these chimes acknowledging the four corners, then I pray:

"I ask that the golden light beings, all the past masters and teachers, healers and prophets, and all those who work in the spirit world with the Creator lead and guide me so that I may help those who come to me with ease, clarity, and without infringement, so that they may grow closer to Him, know peace in their hearts, and reclaim their spirit."

The next step is to smudge my room and the prayer vessel in my serenity room. Smudging is a traditional native practice used as a way of clearing and healing, giving thanks, and asking for empowerment for my daily journey, the client's daily journey, and for all those that they love, for all our relations (meaning, all those in this dimension), and all that is. This is done by burning sage. In my room, you will also see plants, candles, crystals, turquoise, a small Buddha, and a jade dragon. There is a Hopi sash on a shelf behind my chair. On this shelf there is also a large rose quartz for harmony and peace, and three turtle ornaments.

The prayer vessel is a cauldron that was gifted to me. When I first saw it, I loved it, but then I realized what people's reactions might be when they see a cauldron . . . so I drifted in prayer, and heard a voice clearly say: *turn a negative into a positive. Make it a prayer vessel.* That's what I did.

How I react to you at the beginning of a session depends on the state you are in. The minute I walk into the reception to greet you, my sensory motor skills immediately activate and I become instantly aware of your emotional state. As we are walking towards my office I may try to lighten the atmosphere, should you be nervous, because humor is a great healer. When you walk in, I invite you to sit down, and then I sit opposite you with nothing dividing us.

JUDY: Relax, I promise my head won't spin.

CLIENT: So, what do you need me to do?

First, I will explain my prayer vessel to you. I'll hand you a Post-it note and ask you to write down something for which you would like me to help you pray. You can write it in any language, just so long as it is not about money. (People often see money as "winning the lottery" rather than asking for the abundance needed to meet their needs and commitments.) Do not sign your name, and fold the note four times so that it remains closed. I do not read the prayers. Then, I ask you to place it in the prayer vessel. Every four months or so, I take all the prayers and burn them in a sacred fire with the help of a native elder. Grandmother Jeorgina Larocque has assisted me with this on several occasions.

At this point, I will explain to you how I proceed with the reading. I could pick up some of your personal history, or I could even pick up some information on someone else that you know. If I pick up any history, or information that belongs to someone else, then I ask you to let me know. You are leading me. It is more of a conversation than a question/answer format. I generally stay within the coming year — twelve to fourteen months — when I do my readings. From time to time, I go a little further. Often, almost immediately, someone you've lost will show up in the room and give me bits and pieces of information that only you would know. This helps to identify the entity. Sometimes, it's more direct and the entity will tell me his or her name, when he or she passed, or may even mention people in your everyday life for validation of his or her presence. Yes, they are always around.

Here's an example of how a session might go from here:

JUDY: I have a great sense of sadness in your heart right now. A child has shown up from the spirit world. Is there any reason why I would have a sense of this child that is an extension of you in this room right away, very determined that I would let you know of his presence?

CLIENT: Well, I don't ever remember losing a cousin or anybody in my life. Nobody mentioned anything.

As you're going through the thinking process, you open to me.

JUDY: Did your mother ever lose a child?

CLIENT: Yes.

JUDY: I have a sense that this is who this child is, and he's identifying himself as an extension of you. He's either a child of this age, a child who died, or was a miscarriage.

CLIENT: My mother had a miscarriage, yes.

JUDY: What I am hearing is that we have to go back to this pain in your heart, this sadness. And as I go there, one of the things I'm feeling very strongly is that we have to address your mother. Why is she so dominant in the reading?

CLIENT: I'm not sure. She's not on my mind.

JUDY: What is the unfinished business in your heart where your mother is concerned? The sadness is related to her.

And so the reading begins. Readings are all different in tone, and all dependent on the individual. No two readings are alike. It's the same principle with baking. You may bake the same apple pie one hundred times, but there's always something a little different, even if all the ingredients are the same. In all cases the readings are very informal. The more laid back, the easier it is for both of us. The entities that appear could also include animals.

Sometimes, you may just need confirmation that there is continuity on the other side. The messages received are an affirmation that can help you to find peace in your heart. Often a client will confide in me about certain occurrences that have taken place after a loved one has passed on. Perhaps someone lost his father in an accident, and he's having a difficult time with it. And perhaps his father used to smoke a special blend of tobacco, and the smell suddenly arises for him out of nowhere. Or perhaps he'll ask a question to his father out loud: "Can you let me know that you're around?" — to which the lights will flicker on and off. Clients are able to share those experiences, which give them a greater sense of validity of the ethereal world.

When I'm acting as a messenger, the sixth sense that we all have kicks in and the doorways to the ethereal world are opened. Tools that are required to help an individual resolve unfinished business may come to the forefront. "Tools" can mean the transference of information through me from the spirit world that only the recipient would understand, leading to resolution. Once I've connected with a client's emotional state, received validation, and the doors have opened, I can gain a sense of the client's physical state. I've had experiences where I've told people outright what medication they are on, and for a fraction of a second, I'll have a sense of the medical problem. It's akin to observing an X-ray.

Healing comes with acknowledgement, and also with tears. There's a Kleenex box beside the client chair because often the tears can flow. The ratio of male to female clients is equal, so it's obvious to me that both genders are on a quest to feel whole and complete, find peace in their hearts, reclaim their spirits, and connect with the ethereal world. This is the first step in the journey.

EXERCISE:
Every morning I say a prayer of thanks, which I want to share with you:

"Creator God, and most sacred heart Jesus, I thank You for a peaceful night and the dawn of a new day. I thank You for the

*sun, the moon, the stars, and all things in the universe. I thank
You for all the oceans, lakes, rivers, and streams and the gifts
that they give us. I thank You for Mother Earth and all the gifts
that she gives us. I thank You for interceding with all the powers that be, and all the medical profession so good moral choices
are made at all times for every man, woman, and child, and
every creature between heaven and earth. I thank you for hearing the Cogis prayers for Mother Earth so that every man,
woman, child, and every creature between heaven and earth
learns to live in peace and harmony, true spirituality, and takes
care of this planet that You've given us. I thank You for taking
care of all those that I know and do not know in the spirit world
that You have taken into Your loving hands. I thank You for all
past masters, teachers, healers, and prophets and all present day
masters, teachers, healers, and prophets that come my way. I
thank You for sending the golden light beings to walk with me,
to enlighten me, to guide me on my daily journey so that I may
have the wisdom I need to assist all those who come to me. I
thank You for the essence of the Buddha permeating the world,
Your Mother walking amongst the people, to bring them closer
to You, and for sending me the four archangels, Gabriel,
Michael, Raphael, and Uriel, as my teachers, my guides, and
my protectors."*

Giving thanks is very important, and is often overlooked in
our daily lives. What are you thankful for?

Conversations with My Maker

As adults, it's important for us to recognize not only what the youth today are going through, but what we ourselves experienced as children and teenagers. By acknowledging our experiences, we can break them down to discover the lessons. It's also important to recognize that the preconditioning we all experience is fear-based; that we are always struggling against fear in our life's journey.

Imagine that the human life is equivalent to that of an oak tree. The old oak dies, having fought off the elements and pollution (fear) for years. Its branches fall to the ground along with the new acorns. We are reborn from the old life into the new.

In the womb, Mother Earth, we are nurtured until we are born into this dimension; a fragile sprout reaching up for the Creator's light. Some of those sprouts choose to continue to grow. Others die, returning to the earth to be reborn at another time. Such are the children lost in miscarriages. For those sprouts that continue to grow, how long, strong, and tall they get depends on how well they weather the environment. In the case of human beings, we struggle with fear in its many forms. We can get lost in the fear, forgetting to simply look for the Creator's light. While the light is not easy to see, it is always present.

When I was growing up, fear came in many forms: my parents, the Catholic Church, and even at times, the ethereal. This was the beginning of my own journey through life.

I was born in Saint John, New Brunswick, in 1946. My parents were married young: mom was seventeen, dad was twenty. When I was three, we left Saint John because my father's work took him to Ottawa. After leaving the armed forces, my father worked for the government, where he remained for thirty years, his final position in the patent department. I was the second eldest of six children: three boys and three girls. I never felt close to my mother as a child, and often wished I was closer to my father, but sitting or cuddling with him was not allowed. The only child that was close to my father as far as physical touch was concerned was my younger sister, the baby of the family.

Both of my parents smoked — and drank.

Most of my memories from childhood that gave me emotional pain or heartache included alcohol. I was a witness to many fights, both physical and verbal, and endured physical punishment as well. As a consequence, I learned to become more withdrawn into myself to a point where I could appear completely emotionless. Someone could physically pound on me and get no response; that's the degree to which I could desensitize myself. While I loved my parents, and continue to love them, I eventually learned that I did not need to love their behavior or agree with their perspective on life.

When I was a child, I was sexually molested by one of my

uncles. At the time it was occurring, I had separated myself from the experience. I can remember sitting at the foot of the bed playing with a little black rubber doll I had received for Christmas while watching this uncle and myself. It definitely would have been identified as a disassociation experience by the medical profession. The molestation went on for quite a period of time and I never said anything to anyone. At this time, we had a babysitter who would take care of us fairly frequently. One night, I mentioned it to her and I guess she told my mother. My father confronted this uncle, telling him to leave, for he had been staying in our home. Yet there was no sense of justice as the years went by. I began to understand what this uncle had really done to me over several months. After everything that had occurred, it still didn't prevent that same man from coming around with his family and his wife to visit as though nothing had happened. It tormented me for many years. I can't say it was about anger or a feeling of injustice. It was more a feeling of "Why?" Why was no one talking? Why was there no discussion? What I remember was the anger and pain that exuded from my mother, which I felt was directed towards me rather than towards the perpetrator.

At that young age, I had an understanding that what was going on wasn't right but I was too frightened to say anything. Then, when I finally did disclose it, I could *feel* all the negative energy. After experiencing the intensity of my mother's anger, I was afraid of that anger and that awful feeling returning, so later, when a similar situation arose, I kept it to myself.

Such is the sensitivity of children. Children can feel things much more strongly than adults because they have not learned to put up the walls that grow over time, thanks to fear-based experiences. Often, parents work to protect their children by not speaking about certain issues, but children still pick up the emotions and often place the blame on themselves.

I was raised Roman Catholic, and was taught by nuns at a French school in lower town Ottawa. I went to extreme measures at times in order to get some attention. When I was about eight years of age, I desperately wanted everybody to like me. I so longed to belong somewhere that one day, when my parents weren't home, I took a lot of my mother's jewelry and gave them as gifts to the other kids at school. When my mother found out, she was furious. I don't think she ever recovered everything. While my action wasn't ideal, my intention was clear: I was looking for appreciation and affection externally as I was constantly feeling berated at home and didn't fit in. That is common for a lot of children who don't feel loved enough within their family. My mother kept telling me that I had a split personality, constantly inferring that I wasn't "right." I would mumble all the time, talking to my Maker, which is probably another reason why they thought I was crazy. That desire for acceptance and love motivated many of my decisions in life.

As a child, I also did a lot of stuff in church to create havoc, especially at Lent when we had to attend daily. I can remember bringing carrots and celery sticks — anything that would make noise — and I would chomp on them loudly. Back then, I used to be very angry at having to go to church, and to confession, which I would debate internally: "Well, if God's supposed to love me unconditionally and know everything, knowing that he gave me the greatest gift — freedom of choice — to grow in this world, how can He say that He's going to get me if I don't confess my sins?" It didn't make sense and, as far as I was concerned, it was nobody's business. I was told I needed to confess as proof of my devotion, but if He was all-knowing, He would already know where He stood in my heart. And yet, I was told if I didn't go, I was going to go to hell, a place depicted as burning fires and great suffering. So, I would go into the confessional box and make up some outrageous stories. After all, I was supposed to confess to God that I did all these awful things, but what can a seven- or eight-year-old really *do*? Not much. Needless to say, I was assigned the rosary on many occasions. The confessional box became entertainment for me, but even so, I suffered through major emotional conflict about it. Through all of this, however, I continued to have private conversations with my Maker. No matter what, I always believed that He was my greatest ally.

In today's world we are being legislated to death. We are constantly having rules implemented, right from the time we get up in the morning. This legislation is created under the pretense that it's "for our own good." In many ways, what the government is doing is taking away our freedom of choice to learn and grow at the speed we need to. So now we have kids who are trying to find themselves, and questioning some of these experiences they're going through. They are constantly bombarded with rules about how they should think and feel; rules that are created, more often than not, out of fear. I have a number of youths who come to see me, saying they feel like they're being drained all the time. Teens are told how they're supposed to think, how they're supposed to react, how they're supposed to live . . . so they're doing everything they can in order to fight this fear. For instance, instead of teaching the children in love and positive example, they are taught in fear, which brings about the youths acting in rebellion and self-destruction.

In our society, fear is the tool used to manipulate the populace. Right from the beginning, fear is present. There is always something in place to support the fear of authority, and I'm using the word "authority" loosely here. Look at what happens to children who have outlandish behavioral problems; there's an immediate labeling and drugs are administered rather than looking for other possible root causes. If you don't agree to have this child tested for a multitude of "disorders," then there are repercussions. Society gets you to become so subservient that you don't listen to your own truth. Instead, you listen to the fear coming at you and that fear then reflects down to the child.

As I was growing up, I became very argumentative about structured religion. I wanted to have the opportunity to experience all the different religions, and find out how they structured their belief systems, because I was always in conflict with some of the teachings that I was raised with and the fears associated with them. I couldn't accept that God's unconditional love was attached to all that fear and control. At the time, it was just not acceptable to be thinking the way that I was. I knew that there was more to this world than what was being presented to me. There was another dimension involved, another reality, another truth. Yet, back then, it was almost as though the presence of any special gifts was akin to the Devil's work. I could not understand it because somewhere inside of me I knew my gifts weren't evil. However, if I came out and said anything to anybody about what I was experiencing with the ethereal, it would be seen in a very negative light.

Hearing voices and seeing visitors went against everything normal, but at times I ended up telling my mother what I was experiencing on an ethereal level anyway. I would blurt out some of the insights even when I didn't fully understand what was taking place. One time, when I was about eight, I told my mother that there was a hole in the kitchen table with the arborite top, but of course the table was fine when I made that statement. Within a few days, during an argument with my mother, my father smashed a heavy ashtray onto the table, which took a chunk out of the center. I remember thinking, "I wasn't wrong after all." Although the event occurred, it was never considered as proof of my gifts.

There was a period of time when I was thirteen or fourteen years old where I would sneak into my parents' room at night when they were asleep because I kept sensing visitors in my bedroom. I would go and lie at the foot of my parents' bed and leave their bedroom before they got up in the morning. There were many other nights where I lay awake in fear because I knew there were others in the room with me. At first it was simply a feeling, and then I would catch glimpses of their shadowy forms. I would spend half the night talking to my Creator, trying to rationalize what was happening. I kept convincing myself that they were probably angels. Children and animals are very sensitive to the ethereal, and often will see things that adults cannot. The problem was, in that day and age, there was no way to find out more about other dimensions.

As kids, my siblings and I had some violent fights. The only thing we had ever witnessed as children was physical violence, so our first reaction was to attack. As a consequence of a fight with my oldest brother, I was taken to the hospital to get stitches just below my left eyebrow. While there, I told my father that I had slipped on the floor and hit the corner of the table. I wouldn't squeal because I'd learnt that the only one I could trust was my Maker. Children frequently mimic what they see and are often products of their environments. In our home, we soon learned that if you protect your siblings, you protect yourself.

School became an issue. The nuns called my parents when I was in grade six because they wanted me to skip grade seven and go straight into grade eight. The principal said I was very bright and that's why I was restless in school. But my mother had issues with putting me in grade eight. She was concerned that I would end up distorted or in trouble, or worse. It was obvious that she did not want it to happen. As a child, listening to this dialogue going on while sitting outside the principal's office, I started thinking, "The school is saying I'm smart but obviously my family doesn't agree, so what's the use in even trying?"

One of the philosophies I developed very young was, if you're going to call me a liar, then that's what I'll be. If you're going to tell me that I'm not smart, well then fine, I'm not smart. So I could literally feel pieces of me closing off and shutting down. By the time I reached grade eight I wasn't showing myself to be that smart anymore. I got through that year by the skin of my teeth. The mind is very powerful. The concept of "I think, therefore I am" holds a lot of weight, especially for impressionable minds. Negative reinforcement brings negative results.

My sense about the other realm being near was growing stronger, and I couldn't share it with anybody. I can remember on several occasions wanting to take my life because of all the confusion, and feeling and believing that I didn't belong. All I wanted to do was go back to my Creator. At the time, I had an uncle who was considering joining the priesthood. He, too, stayed with us for a brief time. One night, when I was babysitting for the neighbor next door, he brought over books on Plato and Socrates for me to read, hoping they might help me through my sadness. I read them and although I can't pretend I understood everything at the time, the gist of what I did pick up reinforced the idea that there was more than just this one world. There were other realms and I wasn't crazy. The problem was, I still couldn't get my hands on anything to help educate me about the ethereal. So I tried very hard to suppress what I was going through. I had not yet learned that these experiences would be lessons that would be blessings later in life.

I have reached a point now where I have absolutely no conflict with any structured religion. I've learned that it doesn't matter how you choose to approach the Creator. There's no wrong or right way. It is *your* spirituality. So I can walk into any religious ceremony, institute, or church today and feel totally comfortable, because the first thing I do, no matter where I am, is connect immediately with the Creator. The outside surroundings mean nothing. I could be sitting in my living room, sitting in my office, sitting in the middle of a field. I could be going for a drive. The minute my mind reaches out to connect my spiritual self with my Creator, I'm linked. The building itself is only symbolic. The true church is really you. The true sense of spiritual knowing is within yourself, and that's the part that's connected with your Maker.

As a teenager, my anger was continuing to grow. I went through episodes where I despised my father because I didn't think he was strong enough. I felt that he should have stopped my mother from acting the way she did; she was always inciting tears, anger, and pain. The thing that pacified me the most was that I could feel nothing. There was a greater force there to protect me.

When it was time for high school, my father decided I should go to an English school to continue my education in a second language. The trouble was that while I could speak and understand English, I couldn't read or write the language properly. So, I had to repeat grade nine. The school brought my parents in again, saying I wasn't academically inclined and recommended that I take a commercial course. There, I would learn how to type and how to file. While listening to this conversation, I remember thinking, "To hell with it, I can't beat this system."

My father fought their recommendation. He had gone through an academic program and so would I. That didn't change the fact that I was barely scraping by in school. By the time I reached grade ten, I was pushing sixteen and I told my parents I wasn't going back. As far as I was concerned I was a dummy and would never amount to anything, so why stay? I had visions of going to work, putting enough money aside, and getting away from everybody. For years I accepted that I was not bright. It wasn't until later in my adult life that I was challenged on my beliefs, and as a consequence, realized that I *was* intelligent. Again, positive reinforcements can bring positive results.

I had much healing to do when I first started on my journey to unconditional love. Taking a good look at the lessons learned in my childhood was the key to unlocking the hidden positives. Just look at today's teenagers, who are on a real self-destruct trip. How many times do you hear: "I don't understand. I hate myself. I hate this. I hate that." Even adults use these statements. Fear breeds hatred, along with the other dark energies that are self-destructive. I work with youths that are eighteen to twenty-five who have amazing gifts and abilities but also an incredible amount of fear and panic. Today's youth are actually trying to teach us to listen and expand our horizons. When we don't listen, they turn to drugs, alcohol, self-mutilation, violence, and suicide because it's their way of absolutely refusing to stay in this world as it is. If my generation can start looking at how to heal themselves, maybe then we can help some of today's children and tomorrow's grandchildren. The more you heal, the more your inner gifts grow, even if you don't fully understand them.

I also work with children. It's important to note that children, when they first come into this world in their innocence, are spontaneous, and very clear in what they feel, think, and have to say. As adults, we have been preconditioned to shut down this spontaneity, this innocence and untainted truth. When children are brought to work with me, they are often still in their spontaneity stage, sharing thoughts and experiences with their parents that are years beyond what we would call normal with regards to their understanding, comprehension, and visual translations. This so amazes the parents that they want to make sure these children remain spontaneous and untainted as they grow up, and that the system doesn't destroy that unconditional love and beauty. I've been blessed with the opportunity of meeting children who have shared memories with me that are far beyond societal expectation. These children are also being protected by their parents so they do not end up inappropriately labeled and medicated. Many parents have chosen home tutoring or private tutoring versus the structured educational system, and if you look around, you'll see even more parents considering these alternatives.

I've been honored with insight from these children when they have shared some of their past experiences. I worked with a young lad of nine years of age who, when he first entered this world of ours, went through mental and emotional atrocities beyond comprehension. He ended up being adopted by a family who immediately became aware of the many gifts that this child was bringing into their home. They allowed that spontaneity and truth to come forward from this child. At some point, they recognized the many lessons that they would be gifted with from this experience and refused to allow the world of Western medicine to taint him.

They brought him to me in order to help him continue on his journey of growth. His family's greatest concern was to make sure that in no way were they inhibiting this child's journey or the lessons that he was bringing forth into this world, and that they were really hearing and seeing what he was presenting to them. Not only did he recall past lives, but he could see spirits. He claimed a cousin kept visiting him, and described the cousin's attire. He also recalled a specific event that had occurred to this cousin, which he would not have learned from his family. The boy's parents actually went on a quest to validate his memories and were amazed at the discoveries.

When I first met this child, I could see how cautious he was to connect with me. The best thing I could do was to let him walk around in my mind for as long as it took for him to realize that I would not try to control or destroy the gifts that he was bringing forth. This, in turn, gifted me not only with knowledge and wisdom but with new tools to interact with my grandchildren, and any other child that crossed my path. The gifts this child brought forth included an affirmation that we can choose to have more than one lifetime to live and grow. An affirmation of yes, this unconditional love, this beautiful ethereal energy does exist, always has, and the world as we know it today is beginning to fill with children who want to bring that beauty into this reality.

Children have such a spontaneous nature that what they say and how they react to individuals and situations hasn't been tainted by fear and preconditioning. Working with children and their parents is a learning experience for me, and a reassuring experience for the youngsters. All they want is to continue to walk their journey in this world and bring about the changes that will lead to a total state of acceptance and unconditional love. Hopefully they will continue on this path, and that my interaction with them will reinforce this journey.

It's not an easy journey, however, for the child or the parents. One of the first things I might say to parents going through challenging lessons with their children, is:

"First, you have to identify where you are at mentally, emotionally, and physically with this situation."

You'd be surprised how many will say: "I'm just so tired."

Well, that's a given. What you're doing is dealing with your child as well as with all the bureaucracy that is out there, while trying to find answers. So you've explained the physical to me — you're tired — and admitted the physical to yourself. Then we get to your emotional state, and many of the parents are very angry. Admitting to the anger is the awareness the parent often reaches: anger with the system, anger with the preoccupation with labeling and overmedication, anger within themselves because they produced a child who has chosen to experience challenging lessons. They go from being angry with the child to being angry with themselves for these feelings towards their child and for their limited ability to help. They're on a treadmill and they don't know what speed it's going at, how to stop it, or how to progress forward. That tells me right away that the parent has developed an awareness of the illusionary methods that are out there to "fix" the problem. They are beginning to face their truth about their thoughts and feelings around the situation. So, we go into some discourse around that, and without giving them any particular answer, I try to give them insights on how they might change some of the obstacles as they see them and how to network with other individuals experiencing similar challenges. I also provide insights on how to develop the courage to stand behind their own convictions while at the risk of being shot down by all the bureaucratic powers that be who have not reached the same state of growth.

Children today are teaching us the "regurgitation" process. In previous generations, our parents held the philosophy that the past should remain in the past, let go of the yesterdays and move forward. But, if you don't take those yesterdays, look at them, chew on them and regurgitate them, you won't learn the lesson. Until then, you won't be able to let it digest properly and continue with your growth. When I look at my own children, where I first noticed the process, and then at their children, who are trying to teach us the process through their interactions, I can see what needs to be fixed and restructured with the system. You can see the battle that this new generation is going through. Those of the older generation, my generation, who are becoming attuned to what is happening, are now trying to implement changes so that this labeling stops. If we can come up with a new manner of teaching today's youth, and accept the lessons they are sharing with us, then we can learn to walk hand in hand as we grow, discover our truths, and reclaim our spirits.

There are some who would probably say I'm an idealist. There are probably others who would say that I show a lot of instability with my thought process. Then there are those who so desperately want to be whole and complete within themselves who will take time to speak with me and venture forth to put together a growth pattern for themselves and their children, which in turn will affect their children's children. Some risk being shunned by doing this. To all those who question me, I give you great thanks because at least I have you thinking and wanting to react in some way. And to all those who come to see me because they want to reclaim their spirit, face their truths, so that their children and their children's children can experience all of those gifts, I give you my gratitude for having the courage to do this.

EXERCISE:

One thing that young children do is speak their truth straight from the heart. The only thing that will never deceive you in this world is your heart, your spirit. The trick is learning to acknowledge that first thought, that first feeling or impression, and honor it. That is one hundred percent your truth. By honoring it, you are honoring yourself. If you start analyzing it, you are slipping back into that preconditioning that is controlled by fear. That brings about all the "what ifs" and the confusion. Trusting your heart allows you to be who you are, which is one step closer to loving yourself unconditionally. The next time you have to make a decision, take a moment to acknowledge that first reaction without analyzing or questioning it. What does it feel like? How difficult is it for you to simply trust that truth without analyzing it? How often do you follow that first gut feeling? How often do you change your mind?

Testing the Waters

People often wonder what I experience when I'm giving a reading. Let's say I'm with a client who has lost someone important to them. Through either imagery or sensation, I will get an idea of what took this person's life. If the person died through being smothered, for a brief second I will have this sense of being smothered, then immediately I dismiss it. I'll tell the client what I have experienced, and ask if it is related to the passing of that individual.

Now suppose I'm sitting with a client who is on an anti-depressant for severe anxiety attacks. I will hear a voice in my inner ear telepathically revealing fragments of this client's history: if the client comes from an abusive background or if there's been severe alcoholism. This allows me to explain to the person that's sitting with me why it is necessary for him to be on this medication at this point in time.

I'll sometimes see visions, or "movie slides" as I call them, for upcoming things that may occur over the next twelve to fourteen months, both in the individual's private and professional world. From time to time, I'll have visions concerning people they care very deeply about. When it comes to intensity, the only time where it is too overwhelming is if, on the rare occasion, I'm with or around people who are so callous that they'd sell their mother's eyes for a dime. If people have that venom inside of them, I pull away because, for that fraction of an instant, I actually feel that intense negative energy. At that point, I just shut off and say, "That's it. I can't go there," and find some excuse to get away from them.

In my readings, I have found some missing people, as well as helped to reunite people who had been put up for adoption with their birth parents. It has all happened through the imaging that I pick up. While I've helped to locate a couple of people over the years, the greatest agenda I find that my clients have is to further their own spiritual growth.

In all cases, I physically experience everything. The minute the sensation comes from another person, I immediately let it go. You have to learn to differentiate between your own emotions and someone else's, and that takes practice. You cannot take ownership for what other people have chosen to feel and experience in their lives. You have to be able to withdraw from the emotion or sensation so that you can deal with the message within.

At the end of the first session, I tell the client to wait until one of the predictions comes to pass before coming to see me again. Once it has, and they call back for another session, we can go deeper. When clients first come to me, they usually aren't looking to become students right away. On a conscious or sub-conscious level, what they're really doing is coming to test the waters. If I know that you, as a client, are sensitive or aware, I won't tell you right away. I will go on with the reading first until we reach a point where somebody you know who has passed on to the spirit world will show up (which happens ninety-nine percent of the time), and I'll go through a description of them. Sometimes it is what they tell me, and sometimes they show me what I need to see. And then, out of the blue, I'll say:

> JUDY: But you know that person is around you because you've seen her before, haven't you?

Most of the time the response to that statement is:

> CLIENT: Yes, I have. How did you know?
>
> JUDY: Well, why are you here? What do you mean, how did I know?

That tends to lighten the situation before we move on.

> JUDY: I know that you're sensitive, that you've felt things or seen things. Do you want to talk about it?

At this point, the client usually starts opening up. Let's say you are ready to learn more about the ethereal. Then I'll turn around and say:

> JUDY: You may wish you could have control over this or learn more about it.
>
> CLIENT: Yes, I'd give anything.

If you are not quite ready, I might recommend certain books to read, then suggest that you check back with me in six months. If you're absolutely ready — and I only take on two or three people at a time because it's a slow process — then I start with the acknowledgement factor. You need to see the truth in the life experiences that you have had, accept them, and forgive yourself. At this stage, I use my gifts to help you. For instance, I had one client who sat down with me, and I knew she was avoiding the issue that was scaring her the most. So I did the reading, and then I threw out:

JUDY: You're pregnant, eh? When's the baby due?
CLIENT: My God! I didn't think you could tell!

And then the door was open and I could go from there. At that point, it became about going through her world, her lifetime, with her and having her recognize the control that fear had on her.

The first thing you want to do is acknowledge everything. Acknowledge that yes, I hated this person and I wanted to hurt them, or, I was deeply hurt by this person's behavior and I felt devastated. You have to deal with those emotions and recognize that it's human nature to feel these things. What does not help is keeping it all inside, never looking at it, and never finding the positive lesson. Going through the different issues can be a slow process depending on someone's age and experience.

With children, I approach the matter a bit differently. A lot of the time, they'll get to the point where they'll blurt out something.

CHILD: My father's never home.
JUDY: Okay. What are your feelings about that?
CHILD: Nothing. I don't care anyway.
JUDY: Well, that's not true. You're really feeling angry, and scared.
CHILD: How did you know that?
JUDY: Let's just say I know.

I know because I'm feeling their emotions. For some individuals, feeling negative emotions becomes a vicious circle. You are angry at your parents. Then, you begin to hate yourself for feeling this way. Next, you start to resent your parents for making you feel upset with yourself. It's a cycle that goes on and on. So you just have to peel all the layers and get down to the core emotion, and release it. It's difficult to acknowledge the positive sometimes in what we perceive to be a negative experience. Let's take the example of a woman who was molested as a child. In that case, I have heard:

WOMAN: Okay, let's say that I have invited this situation on an unconscious level. But it's still garbage. It didn't have to happen. Why did it happen?

JUDY: Well, look at it this way. Before you came to this dimension, you may have contracted to experience this scenario. Out of this, there is a positive. There's a positive in every negative.

WOMAN: I can't think of anything.

JUDY: You can't think of any positive? All right, what did you learn from the experience?

WOMAN: I didn't learn anything except that I hate this person.

So, it's time to look at it from a different angle.

JUDY: Do you have children? What's the first thing you want to do for your children? How do you want to protect them?

WOMAN: I'd never want them to go through that! So help me I'd shoot anyone if they tried to touch my children.

JUDY: Ah, so can you sense when someone's intentions

are not honorable?

WOMAN: I can smell them. I can tell right away.

JUDY: So what did you learn here? What are some of the positives here?

WOMAN: Oh, so I did learn something.

JUDY: And this person that hurt you doesn't even realize that he gave you this ability, this gift.

So stop and think about it. If you want to open up other doorways and peel off more layers, then you need to look at your yesterdays, find the lessons, and forgive. It could take six months or five years. You've got to be patient.

EXERCISE:

Most of us are caught up in our daily routine in this world. We get swept into the momentum of rush rush rush rush as we begin our day. Set aside fifteen to thirty minutes in the morning, after your breakfast and coffee, after you've taken time to get dressed and face the day, to sit quietly and write down a minimum of six things from the previous day that were either an accomplishment, a pleasure, or a thankful gift. It is a way of honoring yourself by beginning your day on a positive note before you walk out the front door. I personally start my day by writing in my journal and giving thanks for a peaceful night and the dawn of a new day.

The Good, the Bad, and the Uglies

From ages eighteen to twenty-five, individuals who have survived the vulnerable state of growth from sprout to young tree are now frantic about protecting their spirit. They have fewer branches than their adult counterparts, but they have begun to grow their own leaves, which represent the lessons.

All your experiences stay in a memory center. That's from where you draw your wisdom. It's like a large library or storage unit. You have the option of opening the door and going in, pulling out the wisdom from any given situation at any given time and using it in a positive, non-infringing way. Then, your spiritual growth is continuous. If you choose to leave that door closed, your portfolio of experiences just continues to build. If you don't acknowledge what you've learned, you don't draw on the wisdom from that great big library, and you just keep repeating some of the same experiences. However, the lessons become stronger each time, and in a lot of cases, more challenging.

Let's look at it this way. Perhaps you witnessed your parents taking drugs when you were growing up, and you also experienced the effect that behavior had on everyone in that scenario, including yourself. If you store the experience in the memory center library and close the door without looking at it and learning from it, you cannot move forward. Then, when you're older, you end up dating, or even marrying someone who is involved with drugs. Even worse, you yourself get into drugs. You could be stuck in this pattern for years until you finally get to a point where you walk away from it and say: "Okay, I'm going to do something. I don't want to be involved in this anymore."

But again, you don't look at the experience for the lessons. You don't acknowledge the pain from the past. If you keep yourself in denial, you may find you end up with a new partner involved in drugs. The longer you put off learning from your experiences, the more difficult the scenario becomes. At this point, you're older. You've gone through a myriad of trials that are still in your memory center. Then, all of a sudden you wake up one day and you're forty. You feel mentally, emotionally, and physically defeated. That's why it's common for people between the ages of thirty and fifty to sit back and say, "I'm done," and do nothing. Talk about human robotics! You function every day just like a machine. You can't say you're happy, you can't say you're content. . . . All you're doing is going through the motions. There's no *life* in your life. Your spirit suffers because you've taken it and decided to throw it away. I believe that's why there are so many mental institutions filled with people today. People just quit. That's one way of locking the library door and saying: "I don't want to go back into any type of reality because I've chosen not to deal with the truth."

And by not dealing with your truth, which helps you grow spiritually, you certainly haven't grown ethereally. At that stage, you end up in this abyss of nothingness that you're stuck in. That's exactly why some people escape to drugs and alcohol: because it's nice and safe, so they believe.

To grow takes courage. A lot of courage. Fear has created all the "what ifs" in the world. There's got to be a moment where you decide whether you're going to get on with the act of living, or get on with the act of dying. You can choose the quick way and go shoot yourself, or you can do it the slow way with alcohol, drugs, or whatever means you decide to use to sustain this abyss of nothingness. And as you're slowly dying bit by bit every day, you're helping everyone and everything that's around you to die a little bit too. If you can find the courage to take that first baby step and start dealing with your inner truths, then you're going to turn around and end up giving something back to all those who you profess you love, but most of all, *yourself.*

I've heard people say how they love someone so much that they would die for this person. Well, if you stop and think about it, if you're staying in this abyss of nothingness and not facing your demons and your fears, not exploring your inner truth and reclaiming your spirit, then you only *think* you love this person to this degree. It's impossible to truly love another to that degree without unconditionally loving yourself first. That is part of the cycle. Take one step at a time until you are at the ethereal level you choose to be in. By following this, you could possibly reach great heights. Gandhi, for example, kept recognizing his truth and kept growing ethereally and spiritually. To this day he is remembered for his goodness, his caring, and his loving. What greater gift can you give to yourself and to mankind? There is none. What greater gift can you give your children and your children's children? Absolutely none. But you have to start with yourself.

Some of my greatest lessons about fear included my experiences with my first husband, Ivan. I left home at eighteen to marry Ivan, but I certainly wasn't worldly enough. To me, it was an escape route. I didn't fully understand it at the time, but the marriage afforded me the freedom to walk away from the structured religion that I was raised in, and all the taboos and fears that had been drilled into me about my gifts. And even though I didn't like a lot of the "uglies" I experienced in that marriage, they helped me to learn.

I met Ivan at a neighbor's house when I was still living with my parents. He wasn't a tall man, but he was like a rock. Right away we hit it off. Three months later, Ivan came over while my parents were out and I was babysitting my younger sister. When they returned home, only Mom came inside. Dad remained in the car. It was obvious that Mom had been drinking. She stood in the kitchen and started arguing with Ivan. Mom kept asking if he had gotten his previous girlfriend pregnant. I can't remember all the words that were exchanged, but it got ugly.

"Well if you're speaking the truth you won't be afraid to give me her phone number," she said.

Ivan rattled off the number once. She went to the phone and dialed. To this day, his ex-girlfriend has not gotten over the nerve of my mother, calling her up at that time of night to find out if she was ever pregnant by Ivan — which she wasn't. A verbal confrontation ensued, and Mom told Ivan to get out of the house.

"If you throw him out, I'm leaving too," I said.

Dad was still in the car. Ivan made his way to the door and I went with him. She stood between him and me, grabbed him by the shirt, and ripped it. Hearing the commotion, my father got out of the car. He wanted to know what was going on, but by then I had already run to Ivan's car.

"Judy, Judy, come back!" he shouted.

"No, I'm leaving and I'm never coming back!" I said.

That night, I stayed with Ivan at his parents' home. We arranged to get married in a little room in the basement of the church of St. Francis. I had met him around the 12th of February, 1965, and married him by May 22nd of that same year. The priest initially tried to talk me into getting a place of my own, telling me I didn't have to live with my parents. I said no. I was going to marry this rock. Ivan had stood up to my mother! In the meantime, I attempted to speak with my mother on the phone. She kept telling me how I had destroyed my father, knowing I had a weak spot for him. It didn't stop me, though. I went ahead and married Ivan. My parents attended the wedding, along with the uncle who had given me the books on Plato and Socrates. Ivan's father didn't throw money around. He had rented our wedding cake, so I couldn't even eat a piece! After the ceremony, Ivan's older sister gave me a 2x4 block of wood, which confused me.

"That's all Ivan knows. You use that on him, and you'll have a good marriage. It will last."

I thought she was joking.

When I married Ivan, I mistook the illusion of love for the reality of love, which is not uncommon for individuals who feel they have been denied love as children. I believe my intent at that time was for him to protect me. I saw him akin to the Rock of Gibraltar, believing he could shield me from all the uglies of this world and life, and remove them. My plan was to hand over all personal responsibility without taking on any responsibility myself. It was much easier to live in the world of illusion than to deal with truth and reality. That's why the journey between us was very important so that I could learn to recognize this, learn to forgive myself and him, and find all the blessings that came from our union and those experiences.

This marriage was one of the greatest lessons on survival and helped me to open up the doorway of the ethereal world. With Ivan, I didn't have to pretend I didn't see or hear anything. At one point, I said something to him that came to pass within a few days. After that, he bragged about my ability to all his friends. This caused more and more people to show up looking for insights, and that's how it began. Now that I was free to open up about my gifts, I started to do what came naturally and connect with the ethereal. I had the opportunity to experience the freedom of traveling in both worlds and was able to notice the different layers of onion skin between them.

My marriage was far from ideal, however. Ivan was violent when he drank, and I was terrified of him. I got pregnant right away, even though I was on birth control pills. In my mind, I imagined a little doll that I would be able to take care of, and this little doll was *not* going to go through what I went through. While I was thrilled about having a baby, my husband was not. During the pregnancy, Ivan got sick, and we were just leaving the house so I could take him to the doctor when suddenly, I felt wet.

"Oh my God, I just peed my pants."

I ran into the bathroom and dropped my pants, then I saw the blood. I felt myself open and something falling out of me into the toilet. I didn't realize what it was until I stood up and cried out. Ivan ran to the door, looked in the toilet bowl, then flushed. He noticed how much I was bleeding.

"I guess I'd better get *you* to the hospital," he said.

When we got there, I was put between two rubber sheets with ice packed on me so the blood would clot. I was psychologically traumatized as a consequence of the miscarriage. After that, Ivan wanted me to go back on the Pill. It was the first of many miscarriages. I lost three more children between Vivian and my second daughter, Rachel.

These instances stayed buried within me for many years. In the 1990s, I started seeing a psychologist named Brenda. She was recommended to me through a family member who had crossed her path, and not only was I very comfortable with her but I loved the way she worked. She would walk with me, letting me go at my own pace. With each memory I brought forward, she would say:

"How do you feel about that?"

Well, you can express how you feel about it presently, but you can also recall how you felt *at that moment.* And often, what I was feeling at this moment was exactly how I had felt in the past. For example, all the children that I had lost, I had wanted so desperately. I had stifled that loss, but I had been conscious of it for a great number of years. Brenda had asked me if I ever questioned why I had lost all those children. I wondered if it had anything to do with unresolved issues in another lifetime, but then decided it was inconsequential. I am a great believer in freedom of choice, and I felt that those children chose to leave. Then she asked me what I would like to do about it. I had not allowed myself the right to mourn so we eventually held our own memorial service. I recognized how I was feeling about each loss, then acknowledged all of the children, and allowed myself the right to feel them, touch them, and let them go, which was a beautiful experience. After acknowledging the pain and grief, I found a new peace and knew it was okay. As a consequence, countless layers of onion skin peeled away.

When we experience such losses in life, there is a tendency to push the pain aside, or bury it and move on in the hopes that it will disappear. When you're caught up in all the chaos of yesterday's pain and you don't deal with it, you begin to break physically. In my first marriage, my health was so bad that I couldn't even get life insurance. I had developed ulcers that lasted for seven years because of the stress I was under. It was probably in my late thirties when I truly began to under-stand the physical impact all the yesterdays had had on me.

When I was young, I used to love singing, but I wasn't allowed to pursue it professionally because "only tramps sang on stage." With Ivan, there was nothing stopping me. One day, Ivan brought me to the Chamberlain Hotel to meet a per-former friend of his. He arranged for me to sing with him and it started from there. I'd sing every weekend: country and blues in both French and English. I used to have bookings at different places. It wasn't an issue for Ivan because I was in the limelight and it fed his ego. While I was singing, he was drinking beer after beer, on top of the rye that he had had at home. At that point, he would get mouthy and want to fight. I married the nightmare I thought I had gotten away from. Ivan was able to slap me across the face with no hint of a bruise on the outside, but split open the inside of my mouth a quarter of an inch. It was like there were two parts to me: the part that dealt with the ethereal, the visitors, and my Maker, and this other violent reality.

Ivan knew I didn't drink, but one night he brought some cheap wine home with him. I didn't view wine in the same category of alcohol as rye or beer, which was what I had always been exposed to. Needless to say, I was the one to drink the wine, not him. Later that night, he decided we should go to the hotel with a bunch of his friends, and while there, I had four or five quarts of beer on top of the wine. Consequently, I got alcohol poisoning. I don't remember anything, but when I came out of it, I was lying on the bedroom floor, having been violently sick on myself. My arms were covered in blood from falling against the stucco wall outside of our apartment building. Ivan had just left me there. The next day, sick as I was, he just said, "Now you know what it feels like. You know to keep yourself sober and when to quit drinking."

That was my introduction to alcohol.

Just before we moved to a new apartment, Ivan finally gave in and let me get pregnant. During this pregnancy I ended up developing toxemia very badly. Toxemia causes high blood pressure, water retention, and protein in the urine. It occurs in about eight percent of pregnancies and the way to manage it is through bed rest and delivery as soon as the baby has a good chance of surviving outside the womb. While the exact cause is unknown, it's something that can happen when you're pregnant and don't take care of yourself, which I wasn't. I spent most of that pregnancy in the hospital. I was so weak that I wasn't even allowed to get up and go to the bathroom on my own. On the night of July 16, my labor pains began and I delivered Vivian at 5:39 p.m. the next day. Ivan was nowhere to be found.

Within the first year and a half of being married, I kept noticing a dark figure standing behind my right shoulder. I saw this figure as male and it was very tall, and I did everything to pretend it wasn't there. I wouldn't turn to look at it. I didn't want to hear it. I know now that this dark figure was an ethereal being trying to help me, but at the time I was terrified. There was always an urgency behind his words:

"Get out of this, get out of this, get out of this."

Another voice inside me said, "You made your bed, you lie in it." That was the philosophy with which I was raised. My mother said I shouldn't have married him, and leaving him would make my mother right. I couldn't let her be right. So I refused to acknowledge the message this visitor was conveying to me.

We moved to a house on the lake in Carleton Place, just outside of Ottawa. Carleton Place is like any small town with its own idiosyncrasies. The population was about five thousand at the time. The house was in the process of renovation, and I lived for years with no cupboards in the kitchen, unfinished floors, and exposed 2x4s dividing each room.

I decided to refuse to acknowledge thoughts or memories. I thought it was best to be emotionless and not to deal with anything inside of me. I can honestly say I thrived on real fear. Even after my horrible experience with wine, I tried the escape route with alcohol because I wanted to obliterate everything and live in this fantasy world. However, when I say I was ill when I tried drinking, I *was*. My body, both physically and psychologically, rejected alcohol.

Fear controls you, distorts you, and can bring you to a point where it dominates your life to such a degree that you end up committing a ritual form of suicide by mentally and emotionally shutting yourself off until you begin to break down. It takes a while before you begin to see what you're doing. While I had been controlled by fear, it also fueled me to go on a search for knowledge on every level, looking at every topic that was humanly possible because I wanted *to know*. There is no greater teacher than walking the roads of life. No greater gift will feed your insight than walking these roads. In the end, you have two options: you can either let fear control you and continue to eat away and destroy you inside, or you can find a way through forgiveness to let it go. It's a very human trait to punish ourselves for feeling a certain emotion that we may not want to feel. We have to live on the human plateau and deal with all the foibles that go with it.

Somewhere between age twenty-one and twenty-five, before the birth of my second daughter, Rachel, in 1971, an organization that was studying the metaphysical or paranormal approached me. That was my first encounter with a large group of people with diversified gifts. What struck me was that I wasn't peculiar. What drove me to participate was one of the statements made to me when I was approached. The woman said that she knew I was afraid and wanted some answers about my gifts. Of course I did.

The organization had designed a special bed that worked with the theory that the magnetic pull of the earth had something to do with higher psychic awareness. The idea was for the subject to lie on the bed for twenty minutes at a time to see if it had any influence on their gifts. Because they weren't sure what the impact of the bed would be, there were limited time increments for each subject. I was afraid to go on this bed because I didn't know what to expect, so I asked my Maker to help me move beyond the fear.

Almost immediately after the bed began to do its thing, a beautiful visitor appeared. I associated this visitor with Mary, mother of the prophet Jesus. She was of average height, around five-foot-five inches tall. Her shoulder length hair was a light brown to a dirty blond, but I could only see part of it because she had a scarf on. She was dressed in a plain robe, but I can vividly remember the color blue. All she did was hold my hand while I was on the bed. She sat on the edge just holding my hand and smiling, and I wasn't afraid anymore.

I also had an EKG done. One thing the researchers kept commenting on was my alpha rhythm. It appeared as though I was asleep. They also told me, after doing skull X-rays, that I had an abnormally large skull. By the time I went through all of this, I began to realize that this was more of a scientific study. They obviously didn't have any answers. They were just trying out all sorts of theories. I wasn't interested in a scientific explanation because I linked my gifts to my Creator, so I decided not to stay with the group for very long.

From a very young age, I made sure my children and I had our "special times" because I was working so often. I would take a bath with my kids and we'd talk, blow bubbles, do all kinds of silly things. One time, when Vivian was about four years of age, we were sitting in the tub and she started telling me about Daddy having a nap with the babysitter and the games she watched them play. This, of course, led to a major confrontation. I told Ivan that I didn't care what he did to me, but he *wasn't doing anything to the kids*. I threw the babysitter out. His way of getting her back in the house was to badger me mentally, emotionally, and physically until I finally said, "Fine. Do what you want. I don't care."

It was a matter of survival. In the meantime I was focused on protecting my daughters. In this marriage, I had no rights or control over anything. I had to sign my paycheck over to my husband. Because he couldn't read proper English, I had to teach him how to read or I wasn't allowed to have the news-paper. I received six dollars a month as my baby bonus back then, and that was the amount needed to get a phone. If I wanted a phone in the house, I had to sign my baby bonus over to him. When I sang on stage, I would watch him as he approached girls in the bar. He had absolutely no shame. The whole community knew what he was doing. So, I put on rose-colored glasses, not wanting to see the truth because it was too painful.

The mind can be a powerful tool when you take your thoughts and transfer that energy to do something productive or destructive. I had one experience when I was in my early twenties where I realized just what I was capable of. We hadn't been in Carleton Place long at this point. Ivan was taking off again with one of his buddies, and I was so angry. I told them that if they tried to leave, they would never reach their destination. I'd *see to it*. He took off with his friend anyway. After they left, I could feel this rage building. It was an accumulation of all the suppressed anger from everything I had been subjected to. I mentally sent out the thought that I wanted to see them end up in a head-on crash. The amount of wrath and hatred I was feeling was so intense, I felt ready to pass out. I heard a voice saying: *"What are you doing? What are you doing?"*

I stopped my thoughts and immediately got in the shower to calm myself down. Ivan and his friend were back within the hour and they were both ashen. They told me that they couldn't believe what had just happened to them. Ivan had a lead foot on the highway, and was traveling pretty fast. They had been driving for about half an hour when suddenly it seemed as though the vehicle had a mind of its own. It literally picked itself up and half-turned, directly moving towards a rock cut. Ivan just covered his face and thought, "This is it." An instant later, he said he felt the car give a jerk and set itself down. He told me that they were so close to the rock cut you couldn't put a person between it and the front of the vehicle. That must have been the moment where I changed my mind, saying "No, no, no. Don't let me do this," and went to have the shower. After they related the story, I didn't say a word to them, but immediately went off to have a conversation with my Maker. I asked Him that if I ever tried to use whatever gifts I have to hurt anybody out of anger or hatred, that I wanted Him to take them away and never let them come back again. That was one experience that really brought it home to me the power of the mind and what you could do with it.

It's important to look at each individual event as you recall it in its entirety in order to understand its truth and not to push it away, because whatever it was, it affected you in this world. I had experienced hatred and the power it can have when used with the mind, but also learned that I never wanted to experience such venom again. This is where I truly began to know that you have to totally acknowledge the good, the bad, and the uglies to the very depths of your core, of your spirit. Then it becomes about acceptance. There's nothing that could ever wipe it away because it was an actual event that occurred. Then it's about forgiveness, beginning with yourself, because if you can't forgive yourself, you are incapable of forgiving someone else.

At one point with Ivan, I remember thinking of taking my life because I was so tired and afraid, but I didn't have the strength to leave. All the while, a voice kept saying:

"Go, go, go. Do not stay, do not stay."

Ivan had made it clear that if I was ever to leave him, he would hunt me down and find me. My greatest fear was that he would touch my daughters. Fear kept me paralyzed, as it does to many individuals caught in an abusive relationship. Breaking free of such bondage takes great strength and courage, and for many, it takes years to finally do so.

While Rachel was too young to witness things, Vivian, six years older than Rachel, did see some of the physical abuse, and how I didn't have the courage to fight back. I remembered how much anger I had felt towards my father, wondering why he wouldn't take us away from our mother. I could see the pre-conditioning, and I understood. It is common for children with abusive backgrounds to find themselves in abusive relationships. I was not the only one in my family to experience such a violent relationship. As I said, however, there comes a point when enough is enough. Finally, I reached that point.

Ivan always came home at three o'clock in the afternoon after fulfilling his duties as a sanitary engineer. When he got home, the ritual included getting him some coffee, which I would set on the kitchen table. Even after years of being there, we still had no kitchen cupboards, so there was a lot of stuff piled on top of the fridge. On this particular day, the weather was warm and my children were at the new babysitter's house.

For years I could not recall what was said that day. The only thing I could remember was jumping up and backhanding the top of the fridge with my arm. And when I came out of it I was sitting on the bathroom floor wearing a winter coat and sobbing, exhausted. I knew *something* had taken place. I could see marks on my hands and a big leather belt with this huge buckle beside me in the bathroom. I picked it up, looked at it, and started getting flashes of violence. I made myself get up from the bathroom floor, and walked into the kitchen. I couldn't believe the damage. Some of the 2x4 wood frames were smashed. My husband's vehicle was not outside, and he was gone. When I looked out the window and saw my neighbors standing outside watching my house, I called my physician right away.

"I think I did some terrible things and I can't remember. I went nuts and . . ."

"Can you get a neighbor to bring you to my office?" he asked.

So I did. The neighbor that drove me to my doctor's said she had never seen me so enraged. My neighbors knew my husband was rough, and couldn't believe the absolute fear that he had shown while running from the house. They could see that he had been battered. He had to get into the car to get away from me. I had even done damage to the car while he was trying to escape.

I went into my doctor's office and he saw me immediately. I told him about the flashes, what I was seeing, and what was taking place in the images. The doctor had an idea of some of the abuse I had been going through, because at previous appointments I had bruises on my body. He told me that the mind is like a computer: it sometimes reaches a point where it goes into overload. Then, the computer shuts down.

"That's what happened to you," he said.

For twenty minutes he tried to get me to recall what had triggered this tremendous violence. The flashes that I was having included the belt buckle. I saw the leather belt wrapped around my hand, and myself beating Ivan with the buckle. I saw his fist coming at me, hitting me on the side of the head. The fist connected then came right back again. I had flashes of beating him some more, then of holding a sledgehammer with the intent to kill. I could remember being outside but I couldn't recollect seeing the neighbors. Even after I pieced together some flashes, I still couldn't pinpoint what had triggered the outbreak. All I could remember was fixing a coffee and sitting down. We started to talk. That was it. The doctor explained that I had experienced momentary insanity.

It took me at least fifteen years to recall what actually took place. I gave Ivan his coffee and we sat down. Now, my oldest daughter was very well endowed by the time she was nine. He had made a joke regarding her blooming sexuality and taking her virginity when suddenly all my yesterdays came forward. I had always said that you could do what you wanted to me, but there was *no way* anyone would touch my kids. My husband's comment obviously pushed me over the edge.

Ivan didn't return to the house until late that night. My children had shown up at the regular time — early evening. Up to that point, I spent my time cleaning up the house and tried to act as normal as I could. When they arrived, I told them that their father was working. When he showed up later that night, I told him point blank that I didn't want him there, I couldn't live with him anymore, and I wanted him gone. It was over. The violence from that afternoon was still fresh in his mind so he left.

The next morning, Ivan — who was never one to send flowers — sent me this large bouquet. The delivery man gave them to me at the door and I returned inside. After a moment, I let them crash to the ground.

"No way," I thought.

I moved out at once with the kids to stay with some friends. All I took was clothing. Ivan tried coming to see me there but I would have nothing to do with him. Without delay,

I wrote a letter to ensure that my children would go to some-body else should something happen to me. I saw a lawyer, revealed some of the incidents, and petitioned for separation. This was 1975 so there was no such thing as family reform law. I was separated and divorced all within six months. Now, in my mind, my first husband always had two religions: sex and money. I gave him everything on the condition that he gave me sole custody, signed an immediate divorce, and admitted to some of his actions. He consented, and I had to agree that he didn't have to pay more than twenty-five dollars a month for child support. I got sole custody of my daughters for a dollar apiece. He got the house, the cars, and everything else. I had spent ten years of my life with Ivan.

After I left, I didn't inform my parents. I ended up getting a two-bedroom apartment in Carleton Place for next to nothing. I made sure that whatever money I was earning was going towards the rent and food for the girls. With little leftover, I wasn't eating well. My family, who were now also living in Carleton Place, found out through somebody else that I was on my own and came to see me.

"Why didn't you tell us?" they asked.

I said I didn't want to discuss it. I don't know if it was the way I responded, or the look on my face, but they left it alone. My daughters were happy with the new situation. Ivan ended up living with the last woman he had brought into our house. He said that he wanted to see the kids, but then wouldn't show up for pre-arranged visits. He was very involved with his girl-friend's family. His own children took second place.

One of the things I learned from this marriage was how to

become ultra-sensitive to people's moods, to their body language. Ivan helped me learn how to cope with whatever I was faced with; how to work twenty-four hours a day if necessary; how to manage my home and protect my children. I learned how to live on only two meals a day with only a roof over our heads. When it came to sex, I was fairly ignorant when I first left home, but got quite the education with Ivan. I also learned another lesson about alcohol; the effect that it had on me, and others. Ivan also gave me my first chance to discover my breaking point.

The fear that was controlling me stole my spirit. I had seen myself become so subservient that it was a form of suicide. Some of my experiences in my first marriage were good, but for the most part they were as negative as when I was living at home with my parents. The two greatest things that came from my years with Ivan were my two beautiful daughters.

Some lessons I learned immediately, while others took longer to digest. One thing was certain: I knew never to subject myself to physical violence ever again. Also, I knew to never again turn around and use my gifts to perform an act of vengeance. I continued to give readings for friends while I was married to Ivan, and in all cases the people came to me through word of mouth. I had the opportunity to read freely without any fear of repercussions, and the freedom to grow and explore as far as my gifts were concerned. With Ivan, I never had to worry about being punished for my abilities, so I was able to be more spontaneous with them. I learned not to compromise my physical being by walking a path of self-destruction. I learned to forgive, and that it was okay to separate myself from those people or situations that didn't fit the criteria of who I was as a whole. I did grow from the experience.

After leaving Ivan and starting a life on my own with the kids, I became aware of how much fear I really had inside me. I was afraid of everything, determined not to get involved with anybody that didn't mean well or want to take care of us. As far as I was concerned we were a unit. The bottom line was, no matter what was going on, I had to protect the children.

On your life's journey, if you don't learn from what's going on, the same life lessons keep surfacing and the impact grows until BANG! You come to realize something needs to change, and you change it. The question is, how many times will you allow yourself to go through the experience? Once you've decided to change, what's the first step? This is where Brenda helped me. My experiences working with Brenda had a profound impact on my life. Brenda is a fully qualified psychologist with many degrees, but she does not "go by the book." Instead, she walks with you in whatever direction you need in order for you to reach your truth. She's not one of these people who will impose answers, rather she lets you see it for yourself. She would bring me to that point where I had a choice, and the choice was always mine. If you are searching out someone to help you on the next steps of your journey, it is paramount to find somebody who operates within the same principles and perimeters that you're comfortable with. When you don't have that comfort, then the person is obviously not the right one for you to work with.

Now, Brenda walked with me through every aspect of my life as far back as my memory would allow me to recall. I made it all the way back to three years of age, remembering various snippets. Then, we progressed to a point where I was able to recall things at an even earlier age.

One time, we sat outside on the deck by Brenda's office. We talked about healing my inner child, but starting from infancy. She had me take little baby Judy in my arms, and that was probably the moment where I began to love and forgive myself. In my mind, I had much to forgive. That's when I saw all the lessons as beautiful tools I could use to help people. I remember often leaving Brenda's office feeling lighter, as if I were walking on air. It was such a beautiful experience. I learned that the ultimate act of forgiving myself is the ultimate act of unconditional love.

I had an experience that I kept to myself for years, but will share now. My office is in a health and beauty spa. Normally when I have an appointment with a client, I will go forth to the common area and greet my client. As I have said, I have lost many children to miscarriages. If there are any children or babies around, I will automatically go and acknowledge them, and want to touch and hold them. I walked out one day and a woman was sitting there waiting for an appointment that had nothing to do with me, and she was holding an infant wrapped in a blanket. I approached her.

"How old is your baby?" I asked.

"Six months old," the mother responded.

"May I hold him?"

She agreed, and I walked towards this child. When she uncovered him, our eyes connected. I was overcome with such a sense of sadness akin to mourning that I found I was unable to actually touch the child. There was an instant recognition of "I know you" and a great sense of grieving in my heart where this child was concerned. I needed to excuse myself and go off into solitude in my office. I had to recognize what had actually transpired in that moment. The tears ran down my cheeks as I came to grips with knowing that I was looking at one of the children that I had lost: one of the children that I had so desperately wanted to have. When my eyes connected with this child's, he let me know immediately. In that moment, the grieving that I was going through was the recognition of having to let this child go on this new journey without interfering. I was being offered the opportunity, if I chose, to hold this child, however briefly, and to know and feel that bond of unconditional love before setting him free. It was a chance to know that no matter how many times we choose to live on this earth, the connection is never severed.

So after allowing myself the luxury of grieving and accepting for approximately half an hour — my own client having seen what happened and choosing to wait — I knew that I wanted to hold the child, then set us both free, and express gratitude for the opportunity. I walked back out, hoping that the mother and child were still there, and sure enough they were. Once again I asked the mother if I could hold her child, and once again she uncovered him. He looked at me with those wondrous eyes and it was almost as if we both knew I had reached this understanding and acceptance. He gave me a beautiful smile, and as I picked him up, he actually reached up, looked into my eyes, and stroked my cheek. The people around me witnessed this and I could sense their awe. I kissed the child on the forehead and on each cheek, kissed his hand, then gave him back to his mother. In my heart, I thanked the Creator for this wonderful gift. I was able to continue that day with my clients, enveloped in this feeling of unconditional love from the Creator and the knowledge of what I had been gifted with in that moment. I was given affirmation that you can recognize those with whom you have shared history.

So while some of our lessons are tough, gifts are always present. You just need to look for them.

EXERCISE:

There is often unfinished business for some clients that come to me. It can either be with someone who has passed, or someone who is living. In the latter case, if you have chosen not to confront the person or the situation face to face, I explain to you that when something has truly ended in this world, it either gets buried or cremated. So, I suggest that you buy an audio or video tape and honor yourself by using this tool as a way of releasing all thoughts, feelings, issues, joy, and pain. Find a place where you can be alone, and bring along either a Dictaphone or a video camera, a cutting board, and a hammer. The next step is to set up the tape in the machine. While you may feel foolish to start, allow yourself to get caught up in the moment. This is an opportunity to say all that is within you: to cry, to cuss, to explain feelings both past and present. More emotions are unearthed as you get into the momentum of this release. When the tape is done, remove it and place it on the cutting board. To cleanse those final feelings still remaining after the exercise, beat the tape with the hammer until there is nothing left except a sense of exhaustion and relief. After you are done, you should immediately burn the tape, or go outside, dig a hole, and bury it. Although you may feel very tired, the finality and closure of that moment brings about a sense of weightlessness within the spirit and a sense of newfound peace.

Unearthing the Lessons

Remember, the more you grow, the more your inner gifts grow *even if you don't fully understand them.* You may say:

CLIENT: I never want to do what you do. I don't want to *know* in the full ethereal sense.

Even so, you still develop a new sense of awareness, peace, and truth within you. The turmoil that has been eating away at you stops and your life becomes one where the simple things have more value. You have the ability to gain perspective on some of the everyday garbage that hits you. There's less panic.

When working with my clients on their journeys, I will often hear resistance. For example:

JUDY: Has there been any kind of mental, emotional, or physical violation that you have endured? Because I have a sense of violation.

CLIENT: Yes, I was raped. But I don't *want* to remember that I was raped.

Then I go further with the conversation, touching on the importance of acknowledgement.

JUDY: You don't want to remember and yet you do. You

remember every day in your thoughts, your actions, and your interactions. And I did not mention the word "rape." What I did ask you was, has there been any kind of mental, emotional, or physical violation? So whether or not you want to admit it, yes, you are remembering, or that wouldn't have been the first response. The first thing you have to do is acknowledge the truth of this moment.

Then I begin to walk with them. Now, I see clients who have *a lot* of mental and emotional garbage that they have to get through. I don't presume that I can lead them through all of this. If I perceive a real physical illness, or a large amount of psychological pain, I'll refer them to a medical professional who is open to homeopathic techniques; somebody who will give them the proper aid that they need because I don't pretend to have that expertise. You must remember, however, that the person I will send them to is someone who has true empathy. After many of these clients have finished their journey with a professional, a lot of them will come back and see me. At this point, some are ready to delve deeper. Others will say:

CLIENT: I've dealt with the first part, and I'm aware of the ethereal, but I don't want to go beyond where I am now. I don't want to walk in your shoes. I'm happy in my skin the way it is now.

And that's fine. They don't have to continue on that path. This is *their* choice. And I always use the word "choice," because choice is one of the greatest gifts. I've had people ask me: "Don't you think you're playing with people's lives by telling them what you see?"

JUDY: No, I'm not, because ultimately, they still have a choice in this matter.

No matter what I sense or what I see, the final choice is yours. You may dismiss everything, ridicule everything, or you may choose to take bits and pieces. You may doubt my words, or wait and see what happens. You're in the driver's seat. There's no right or wrong. Every negative has a positive, and if you can find that positive, you've found the lesson. Some of these lessons are extremely painful, but if you choose to learn from them, you will be able to share the knowledge and wisdom you've gained from the experience with everyone who crosses your path.

You have to realize that when I'm sitting with clients, I'm instructed right from the beginning. Most say I have a very gentle approach, but still very direct. And yes, from time to time, I'll let some clients walk around the topics for the first fifteen minutes because each person is unique. And if it takes an extra twenty minutes for them to be totally who they are within themselves so they can proceed, then that is what occurs. From time to time, there are those who come and I sense and hear: *no*. At that point, I will tell them this is not a good time for them to sit with me. It doesn't happen often, but when it does, I heed exactly what I'm being told. It may be something as simple as my saying to them:

JUDY: You're in the process of making a major decision right now, but I will not choose for you. When you have

57

chosen, then I will see you. For even I will not interfere with your freedom of choice.

I'm just a messenger, and you must acknowledge your right to choose, not look to someone else to make the choice for you. That's one of the most important things that I tell people, as well as that my life is like everybody else's in this world. I have my good, my bad, and my uglies. If I sense that a client is beginning to see me in a different light, the first thing I say is:

JUDY: Hey, I have to sit on the toilet like everybody else. Think about it.

The hardest thing to do is look in the mirror and see those truths. By looking in this mirror, you take control of this fear. Every moment of the day there's something happening in this dimension to breed fear, to breed control, to breed chaos. If you look at the world, how many people are fighting in their own countries, in their own homes, and within themselves about issues that are relatively unimportant?

CLIENT: I don't understand this fully yet. I want to know more.

The first thing, like I said, is to work on facing all those fears and those demons, with the understanding that you'll get to a place where fear no longer controls you. But I have to be clear: fear is always present. If you want to look at it in religious terms, fear is the Devil. That's what triggers all our negative behaviors, reactions, and interactions. The idea is to get beyond it so that you end up in the driver's seat. You know the fear is there, and it's not going away, but you choose not to succumb to it. You choose not to let it dictate your actions and reactions.

This process helps in developing a sense of unconditional love for yourself, which is the direct bond and link with the Creator. Everything comes from the Creator and there are absolutely no uglies there. The minute there's a sense of an ugly inside of you, remember it has nothing to do with the unconditional love and that bond. It has to do with the dimension that you're walking in.

If a client comes to me and says:

CLIENT: I want to learn to talk to the dead.

JUDY: Talk to them, they hear you.

And I go no further. If a client comes to me, however, and says:

CLIENT: I want to connect with a deceased relative that I love a great deal. I want to have a sense of connection on an ethereal level with this person. I want to feel that person. I want to hear that person. I want to be able to touch this person ethereally. I know I can't touch them in the physical sense.

Then I know that this client is truly in search of their truth, that they want to connect to the ethereal plane and heal, and that they'll take the time required and trust that they will succeed.

When it comes to teaching, I won't take anyone on until they are ready to move forward. Sometimes, I may have the same students for a number of years until they reach a point where they know that they can continue the journey on their own. After that, they may come and see me once a year to touch base. I have one student now who is reaching that level. I've worked with him for approximately ten years. Like I said, age is not a real factor. If, by the time you reach twenty, you've lived a life where you've been through a great deal of garbage, it may take several years to get to the next stage. Getting to the positives involves sorting through all the negatives and if you've experienced something painful, it's possible you've put yourself on that treadmill. You hate the person who hurt you, then you hate yourself for hating that person. Then, the circle grows bigger. You end up hating your parents because they didn't protect you. Then you start hating the siblings who didn't have to experience the same trauma. And then you hate the world because nobody understands. That's where all this fear controls you. So the lesson comes after the forgiveness. Okay, you were hurt. Now, what did you learn from that? What positive thing came out of this experience? It's challenging at first, but the more you do it, the easier it will become.

EXERCISE:

I suggest to clients that on their search for their truth, to try to remove all preconditioning from their spirit and to honor all thoughts and emotions without the labels of "good," "bad," "right," or "wrong." They need to acknowledge the complete truth of that emotion or thought so that they can find the lesson and gift that is in there. By doing so, they will be able to release that emotion and will have uncovered a wisdom and a knowing. Each moment takes time. Take a situation in your life and ask yourself: what did I learn from that experience?

Tuition Fees

The oak tree continues growing, still battling to survive, struggling against disease as well as other environmental toxins. More branches are growing, adding more leaves to its foliage. The leaves — the lessons — continue to grow in number. When you look at a tree, its foliage is part of its beauty. Similarly, our life lessons are a part of our beauty as human beings.

If I hadn't decided to walk all these journeys in this lifetime, I wouldn't have the first-hand tools to truly say "I understand." Nor would I have anything to share. Worst of all, I'd be incapable of receiving. To me, the greatest gift I can give someone is total exposure and openness of who I am in this world and my connection with the spirit world. That way, these words can end up being not only a teaching tool for you, but a gift too.

The old statement of "love your enemy, turn the other cheek" holds true if you remember that loving your enemy does not mean that you have to like the behavior exhibited by the person. Once you reach the point where you can truly acknowledge a situation and forgive yourself, you reach acceptance. You can't change what has taken place. It's much easier to avoid getting caught up in the emotion of hatred when you have forgiven yourself, because it doesn't touch you again.

When it comes to readings, I see images. When I have visions, I drift. It's akin to what they call "astral traveling" where you're listening, watching, and partaking in all the things happening in front of you. And then when it is done, you drift right back to the reality of this world. The images are literal. You are there when they're taking place and are very much a part of them. It's like being in a movie and watching the movie at the same time.

When someone shows up for a reading, they usually come back more than once. In the 1970s, I was doing readings two or three times a week for ten to fifteen minutes. My gifts did not, and still don't, hold any special benefits for me when it comes to noting my own future.

I had a whole new sense of inner peace once I was out of the violent scenario with my first husband, and my children were protected. I had a reliable source to take care of them when needed. The shadow that had lingered for so long when I was with Ivan, urging me to leave, had finally gone. I kept working and singing, having developed a new philosophy: I was going to be in control. Any men in my life would be "who I want, where I want, when I want": strictly one-night stands. Things went that way for a few months. Then one day, I heard a gentle voice.

"What are you doing? What are you doing to yourself?"

It guided me to go watch my daughters, who were asleep on their bunk beds. I went into the girls' room, watched them sleep, and was overcome with an amazing sense of love. I realized after that, I wasn't going to be with just any man. In fact, I wasn't going to be with a man at all unless it was heading towards a true, loving relationship.

We still had next to nothing. My mattress was on the floor but I made sure my kids had their bunk beds. I started doing office work, eventually graduating to a big corporation, working in administration.

I first met RJ in May of 1981 at the home of friends of mine. It had been several months since I'd seen them, so I decided to stop in unexpectedly with the kids. When I arrived, they had company. When I was introduced to RJ, I immediately had an overwhelming sense of being caged, boxed in. The first words out of my mouth were:

"You're the most arrogant, egotistical son of a bitch I have ever had the misfortune to meet. Stay the hell away from me."

I left the room and all he did was sit and smile. He never bothered me for the rest of the evening. Now, the uncanny thing was that every time I would stop in to visit these friends, RJ would show up five minutes later. It wasn't because he knew I was coming and pre-arranged it. When he saw my kids, he would charm them, but I still did not like him. RJ ended up asking me out more than once. I would say yes but then stand him up. I just didn't want to have anything to do with him.

One evening, there was a function at a mutual friend's home. RJ was there with his brother. His brother needed a ride home, and RJ asked me to come along and keep him company. As my children were spending the night with a friend, I agreed. We must have driven for about forty-five minutes before dropping off his brother. After, he said: "You know, I'm really tired. I live close by . . . and I've got a guest bedroom. Don't worry. Nothing will go on. I drank a little bit at the party, and it would be better if I didn't have to drive any further. I will get you home tomorrow. What time do you have to pick up the kids?"

"Around nine," I told him.

"I'll have you home in time to pick up the kids."

So I said, "Fine. So long as you have a guest bedroom."

At this point, I was looking at the clock on the dashboard, and it was already two o'clock in the morning. I thought I might as well get a couple hours of sleep. RJ lived in Jasper, which wasn't far from Carleton Place. Sure enough, once inside, he showed me where the guest bedroom was. I went in and shut the door.

I lay in this strange bed in this strange house, twisting and turning. All of my fears were resurfacing. So, I got out of bed. I had only been there for maybe half an hour. I went to use the bathroom then walked out to the living room. I sat on the couch and lit a cigarette, taking a look outside. That's when RJ came in.

"Can't you sleep?"

"No, I can't," I said.

He reached over and took my hand and walked me back to his bedroom. We lay down together. We got up the next morning at seven, had coffee, then drove back to pick up the kids.

Suddenly, RJ knew my hours at work and what time I would come home. When I arrived, he'd be there with groceries; an abundance of everything the kids would want. I finally started seeing him. I was looking at a self-made businessman, working in the retirement and nursing home industry. Any time he wanted to do something extra for me that related to finances, I would refuse. So he did things when I wasn't around. I'd jot everything down, telling him that one way or another, he would get his money back.

One day in October, at about four o'clock in the afternoon, my phone rang about two minutes before I left work. I picked it up.

"Hi," RJ said. "When you drive back to Carleton Place, you're in for a surprise. You don't live there anymore. You now live in Jasper. I'll explain everything when I see you," and he hung up the phone.

"What was that about?" I thought.

I got in the car and drove from Ottawa, where I was working, to Carleton Place. I pulled into my home, unlocked my door . . . and everything I owned was missing. Then the phone call hit me. I rushed to the car and drove all the way to RJ's home in Jasper. My kids came running out shouting, "Mommy, Mommy, don't be mad. We asked RJ to move us. We want to live here. Please Mommy, don't be angry. You don't have to unpack, we'll unpack it all!"

Vivian begged, with young Rachel mimicking her. It went on and on. RJ stood there, looking at me. I didn't say a word. Vivian was crying. "Mom, this is such a nice house. *Please!*"

Although the girls never went hungry, I never had money left over for any extras like toys. For a good time, we would pack a picnic and walk to the beach, but winter was coming and with that, more hard times. All my children knew was that

I was working all the time to make ends meet. I was also trying to do readings for people, but I wasn't charging anyone.
Every once in a while an individual might leave a donation,
and that was a big blessing.

I walked into RJ's house. He had cleaning ladies unpacking
everything and setting things up. He said, "It was the kids who
really wanted me to organize the move. You went to work, and
they were after me to move them."

"Where did they get the idea to start with?" I asked, quietly.

"Well," he said, "I mentioned that eventually I wanted us
to be able to live together and they jumped on it right away. It
was too hard to say no to them. But if you're not happy, Judy
. . . within three or four months, I'll move you back."

"I can't do that to the kids," I said.

"I really want it to work between us . . ." he began.

He said all the right things. I never said anything, never
fought it.

There was no way I would take money from him. I wasn't
going to be beholden to a man or to anyone else when it came
to finances. My need to be fiercely independent came from my
yesterdays. After my first marriage, and before meeting RJ, I
had a two-year relationship with another man. We lived
together, with his children and mine, had just bought a house
and were preparing to move in, when he informed me that he
no longer wanted my children to live with us. There was no
compromise. I took the kids, found a place, and walked away
from the house and the relationship. Once again we were on
our own, but we survived. With RJ, learning to trust and open
up was very difficult. For many people who have experienced

traumatic events, opening up to another can be extremely challenging, especially if the person has not yet acknowledged the hurt and gone through the healing process, which I hadn't.

Shortly after New Year's, RJ proposed marriage for the first time. We had been together for maybe seven to eight months at this point, and when he asked, I laughed.

"I'll take the ring, but it will never happen," I said.

I was determined to never get married again. After that, RJ goaded me to quit working in Ottawa. He suggested that I could help him at the nursing home since I already had some administrative experience. As no one on staff spoke French and he did have some French patients, I could be of assistance. It also meant that I could be around more for the kids. RJ would often bring up stuff like this in front of the kids, and of course they would react with: "Please mom, you'll be home more . . ."

Eventually, I resigned my position. Every day, I would go with him to the nursing home. We never left the house before the kids went to school and were back home before the kids returned. RJ had two children of his own, Sheri and Michael, who lived with their mother, visiting us on weekends. I had no idea about the ins and outs of the nursing home business, and took all of RJ's words as gospel truth, because I had no reason to believe that he was lying. I knew he drank a lot of black coffees, and had a couple of beers a day, but it wasn't an issue because his personality did not change.

One day, RJ came home and physically collapsed. The doctor said it was some form of mental breakdown. RJ wouldn't leave the house. He locked himself in the bedroom. The doctor put him on medication, informing me that his situation was pretty serious. RJ was getting close to forty at the time, and the doctor warned us that if it happened again, RJ might not pull out of it. It would take a while before RJ got his strength back and was thinking clearly enough to return to work. By this point, I was really learning to care for this man. Therefore, RJ gave me power of attorney, signing over all the bank accounts so that I could be responsible for the paychecks and help maintain things. I still had no idea how to run the business and I wasn't getting any direction from him. I was flying by the seat of my pants, especially with the finances. If there was money in an account, whether it was a trust account, a payroll account, or a personal account, RJ instructed me to take the money as a loan whenever we needed it for paychecks, expenses, or personal matters. Then, I would return the money to the account from which I had borrowed it. I ruled with an iron fist, refusing to budge on anything the staff wanted to change because I didn't know any of the rules and regulations. As a consequence, there was a lot of resentment from some of them. After all, I had walked into this place because I was involved with the boss. Thankfully, within a couple of months, RJ was back at work.

We moved into the guest house near the nursing home in the early months of 1982. The guest house was a big old building, larger than our previous house, only there were residents now living downstairs. Four months after the second marriage proposal, which had occurred six months after the first, he called me at the nursing home and asked me if I could come home straight away.

"It's very important," he said in a somber voice.

"Okay, I'll be there right away," I said.

I hung up the phone, but as I was in the middle of calculating something, I got caught up in the math. While still trying to finish things about fifteen minutes later, the phone rang again.

"I thought you were coming right home," RJ said, now sounding *really* somber.

"I'm so sorry, RJ. I'm on my way."

I hung up the phone and left work. When I walked into the home, I asked the woman working in the kitchen where RJ was.

"Upstairs taking a bath," she said.

"*What?* Taking a bath?"

That put my back up immediately. The kids were in the dining area with the residents; they had learned to work with the elderly at a very early age. I went stomping upstairs and as soon as I entered the section where we lived, RJ heard me and shouted my name.

"Where are you?" I asked.

"I'm in the bathroom. Can you get me a suit please? Pick the one you think looks the best on me."

That comment stopped me in my tracks. There had to be something that had happened that he hadn't told me. I went into the bedroom. RJ was in the adjoining bathroom.

"Do you want this suit?" I asked, showing him.

"Yeah, okay." Then, he said, "Pick the best tie to go with it."

After doing all of this, I asked him: "What shirt do you want to wear with it?"

"Well, I'm asking you again. Will you marry me?"

I stopped dead in my tracks then walked to the bathroom

door. Here was this man, sitting in a tub full of bubble bath while I was in a business suit. I walked right up to the tub, holding his shirt, and it struck me as so funny that I burst out laughing.

"You know something?" I said, "Any man who would sit in a tub of water and propose to a woman finally deserves 'Yes' for an answer."

RJ pulled me into the tub with him. Soaking wet, we both changed. This time he didn't have a ring for me.

"I decided not to buy a ring until you said 'yes' next time," he said.

We went downstairs, and he told the children that he had proposed and that I had finally agreed. The plan was to go out to pick my ring. RJ brought me to a jewelry store, and the one I selected fit me perfectly.

"You can't wear it right now," he said. "I want to do this right."

He took me to an ordinary hotel. Inside, he ordered me a glass of wine and a beer for himself.

"I wanted to do this here," he said. "Because of who you are, I wanted to put this ring on your finger in a place that has people from every walk of life."

He put the ring on my finger, again showing me that he had no prejudices or judgment.

Because I did not have a proper wedding the first time, I decided we should go full out for ours.

At this point, we moved out of the guest house to a new place registered in my name in Smith's Falls. I had made the decision after one of the residents that Vivian was close to died right in front of her. The incident devastated Vivian, so I decided a relocation was necessary. We were still very active with the nursing home, however, and as it had its own chapel, I decided that I wanted to get married there with the residents as part of the ceremony. RJ was friends with a minister, who he wanted to officiate the ceremony. There were some complications regarding the jurisdiction of the minister, and as a consequence, we needed to seek permission from the Archbishop. In the end it was decided that we would officially be married in the minister's little parish chapel, with the full ceremony to follow in the nursing home.

The rehearsal took place in the nursing home the night before the wedding. The Reverend called me into the office where my matron of honor, Maggie, RJ, and his best man, Tom, were waiting. As soon as I walked in I knew there was something wrong.

"What's the problem?" I asked.

Reverend Betts just spewed it out at high speed:

"Judy, RJ forgot the marriage license but we can go through all this tomorrow regardless and everybody will think you're married. I can marry you privately within a week at my office and nobody will know the difference."

I hit the top of the desk with my hand.

"As far as I'm concerned," I said, "If this marriage doesn't take place the way it is supposed to tomorrow, it will never happen. It's not *meant* to happen."

I marched home. RJ showed up three hours later and said: "You have to come with us."

My matron of honor's mother was very well connected

with politicians. Apparently, on rare occasions they will give you special dispensation. Over the phone, they provide you with a recorded number that becomes your wedding license number. The number allowed us to go to a notary to have the license signed. In order for this to happen, we had to drive way out of town, but we got everything done. It was about three in the morning when we finally got home.

We got married in the chapel at 2:50 p.m. on June 18, 1983. We had the second ceremony in the chapel at the nursing home with all the residents celebrating with us. We had arranged to have our honeymoon in Montebello, Quebec. That first night we arrived, I was exhausted, but RJ insisted on consummating the marriage. I finally gave in.

The next morning while we were having breakfast, RJ turned to me.

"You want to know why I was so insistent on consummating the marriage?"

"Why?" I asked.

"So you couldn't legally change your mind because the marriage wasn't consummated."

The comment hit me like a sledgehammer, but he went on as though he hadn't said anything. On the third day of our honeymoon, RJ called his nursing home to discover that all the accounts had been frozen. We drove back immediately. That was the moment when we found out that the bank couldn't clear the paychecks and that he was behind on his taxes. All sorts of truths were surfacing.

"Why don't you just sell everything?" I said to him. "Walk away. If the place is worth as much as you were talking about

— four or five million dollars — just sell everything. We can start over someplace else. At least then you'll have a couple million dollars to get a fresh start. You won't have all this garbage."

By then he had revealed to me that his brother and ex-partner had taken some money from the nursing home trust fund while working there, and that he had been working all this time to return it. Before he met me, RJ had owned a trucking company, which he had sold to try to bail out the nursing and retirement homes, which were located side by side. His brother had put them all in jeopardy. Everyone was screwing him, RJ said, and he couldn't trust anyone. On top of all this, he was getting sick again.

"You heard what the doctor said. You can't do this to yourself," I told him. In the meantime, I started to notice that he was caught in a depression and drinking more than before.

"You've got to sell the business. You can't hang on to it," I finally said.

He agreed that he had to get rid of it, and I was under the impression that we would end up with over a million dollars from the sale. A big corporation in Toronto was going to buy him out. In the end, RJ sold the home to a real shark. There was nothing I could do. RJ was growing a lot testier, and I was forever making excuses for him.

Old patterns started emerging. My husband was drinking more. His personality was changing. The signs were there, yet I chose to stay and continue learning these lessons. In the spring of 1985, RJ lost everything. While we still had the house in Smith's Falls as it was in my name, we decided we should sell that as well. The plan was to start over and buy a restaurant in Kemptville, Ontario. RJ said he'd do some short-order cooking for breakfast as well as hire a chef. The restaurant we were looking at buying was quite large, so we could also provide entertainment: I would sing. It would all work out.

I used to let RJ handle the business side of things because I wasn't very business oriented. So my husband managed the sale of my home with another shady character. When I signed the papers for the sale of this home, as far as I knew it was for a set amount and the money would be used to buy the restaurant. But that's not the way it went. When we took over the restaurant, all we had with us was our clothing. When it came time for me to retrieve my belongings from the house in Smith's Falls, we were in for a surprise. All my personal effects were gone. *Everything* had been sold.

We had the restaurant for six months. It was a fine dining establishment called *The Villa Torres*. I had made a very specific rule about the cash: if someone took twenty dollars out, they would have to leave a note as to what the money was taken for and who took it. Despite the rule, we kept having problems with money missing from the cash. I assumed RJ had been paying the GST and other taxes. He hadn't. Eventually, Revenue Canada came to seize the property. Once again, we lost everything. It was late fall of 1985 and we were destitute once more.

Before RJ and I were married, I can remember telling him that he would have only one opportunity to fix things before catastrophe struck, but he did not want to hear it. If he had paid attention to what I had said, he may have saved himself and the others in his life a lot of heartache. But he chose not to. And at the time, I chose to stay in the mess, so obviously there were more lessons for me to learn. I couldn't hold him responsible for the lessons that I chose to experience.

One of the most important things I've learned in all my experiences is *intent*. If you want to cleanse yourself and are taking a shower, that is the intent. In that moment, you can also choose to cleanse your mind, heart, soul, and spirit. Only two people know your intent: you and the Creator.

I was faced with a client one day who carried a crystal. After I explained intent and cleansing, I was asked:

CLIENT: How do you cleanse your crystal?

JUDY: You can use sage, with the intent that all negativity that has accumulated in this crystal be removed, and then once again let it be filled with the Creator's love, light, and healing powers and protection.

CLIENT: What if I have no sage and I cannot buy any sage?

JUDY: Run it under the tap, cleanse it with water.

CLIENT: What if there is no water?

JUDY: Reach down and use Mother Earth.

CLIENT: And what if I'm in an abyss of nothingness where none of these things exist?

JUDY: With the intent of your spirit, hold it in your hands, and in your heart ask for the cleansing.

The important factor is the intent. It is the purest form of unconditional love that is communicated between your spirit and the Creator. You are always functioning on this. When you're born, your intention is to live. When you leave this world, it is with the purpose of living in another realm. The cycle of life is never-ending. Likewise, the journey of finding unconditional love and wisdom never ends. When you hurt yourself, or others, your intentions are fear-based. While the positive leads to unconditional love, fear-based intent only brings, you guessed it, more fear. You have the freedom of choice.

My intent, when I finally married RJ, was to begin to live some of my personal dreams and philosophies and to set aside a lot of yesterday's shadows without dealing with the truth. My union with RJ once again was part reality and part illusion. There was distinct growth there, but it took the rest of that union to face my truths, discover who I was, and develop more wisdom, so that I in turn could share this wisdom with others and continue to develop my ethereal gifts to their highest potential.

I still go through moments where I get down about something, and then I remind myself that it's okay not to like it. I even loathe certain things at times, but the minute that I acknowledge what I'm feeling, I have a new peace inside of myself. I learned to pull back and see the situation from a different perspective. The solutions come when you are not caught up in your emotions, but first you have to acknowledge the emotions because otherwise you're building them up inside. Eventually, you hit an explosion point and the situation never gets resolved properly.

I tell some of my clients, "This dimension is like a giant classroom. When it comes to the concept of 'life education,' there's nothing in this dimension that doesn't have some kind of tuition fee. So the negatives are your tuition fee. It's nothing but a bill that gets paid. Now, what did you learn?"

EXERCISE:

Sometimes, we are so caught up in a situation that it is difficult to see things clearly. When this is the case, I suggest that you fill your bathtub with water, a temperature that you enjoy, bring in several candles or play music at a soft volume that soothes you. Bring in a glass of wine, juice, or water, or a cup of tea, and allow yourself the luxury of drifting and resting in these surroundings. Water is a great conductor of energy. You will be surprised at the clarity that you feel about situations that have taken place during the day. You can unburden yourself and sink into a sense of peace and self-love, just from this simple exercise. When you are relaxed, take another look at the situation. What has changed?

Embracing the Energy

I usually don't teach more than two or three people at any given time (individually), and these people have chosen to work with their gifts and open that doorway. They have gained the understanding that this journey is really theirs, not mine, and they can stop at any given time or reach any level that they choose. I warn them that this is not going to be an easy undertaking. Although I'm not available to connect with them around the clock, that doesn't mean they can't call me if they have a question. I will get back to them as quickly as I can, usually within forty-eight hours. If their question has to do with making choices, I tell them outright that this is something that they have to decide on their own.

If you reach a point where you want an answer, my advice is *listen to your heart.* Should you start analyzing or question that first thought or feeling, then you're slipping into the preconditioning. From your earliest memories, every thought, feeling, experience, and interaction has to be looked at. That isn't an easy journey to take, because you have to look at all the things that were done to you, all the things that you've done to others: good, bad, or indifferent. You have to be able to acknowledge all the bitterness, all the anger, all the jealousies and fears, and you have to be able to do this with unquestionable truth from within. That doesn't mean that you have to speak that truth to me or anyone else. It means you have to speak that truth to yourself.

For instance, your father was an alcoholic and verbally abusive. You always had a sense of never measuring up. You've spent your life to date trying to win his approval and affirmation of his love and pride in you as his child, as a person, and as an adult. But while you were growing up, you hated him for certain things that were said and done, and consequently experienced anger and rage within yourself. You have gone to that moment in time in your truth, acknowledged all that venom, all that pain, all that bitterness. . . . Now you have to be able to look at that negative and find the positive — the lesson. Sometimes there are several lessons in each experience. So, as an adult, when you look at that moment in time and stop holding your father responsible for the choices you have made and are making as an adult, you need to find forgiveness within your heart and come to terms with the fact that we all suffer the limitations of being human. We have chosen these lessons either consciously or unconsciously, from the first breath that we've taken in this world.

It could take months or even years before you've gone through every facet, and that is probably the greatest healing journey you will seek. As you do that, you must allow yourself the time. Regardless of the time it takes, you must have the willingness to look at it all. It's only through accomplishing all this that you begin to open the doorways to your inner gifts.

Only then can you truly experience a fraction of this unconditional love for yourself and reach a state of complete trust of who you are as a human being. At this point, you will find the wisdom that you need in order to help all those who cross your path.

CLIENT: Will the entities tell me what I should do or what choices I should make?

Keeping in mind that the Creator gave us unconditional love and freedom of choice, I'll use an analogy of how the ethereal beings will try to assist:

JUDY: Let's say you had a verbal conflict with your partner. In a temper you grabbed your coat and you thought you'd just take off and go to the mall. As a rule, when you walk into your house, you throw your keys into a bowl by the door. It's a daily ritual, but when you grab your coat and reach for the keys, they're not in the dish. You hunt high and low for ten minutes, and you find the keys on the kitchen counter. Fleetingly, the thought might cross your mind, 'What are they doing there?' But instead of using the past few minutes to diffuse the state of mind you're in, you allow yourself to become angrier because you didn't get the keys right away. So you march out the door to where the car is, and as you reach the vehicle, you notice there's a flat tire. Still, instead of hearing what is being said to you or seeing the message, you allow your emotions to go wild and become angrier. You then run into the house, call a taxi, and take off to the mall. Halfway to the mall, the taxi you're in has a head-on collision and you're seriously injured. You chose your reaction, your state of mind. You chose the lesson in that moment to be that, but the ethereal was there to assist you by giving you options.

When I work with a client for the first time, after I explain all these steps, I ask the client to take time and really digest everything I've said regarding this process. Should the client call me back within a day or two, my feeling is that this person hasn't fully comprehended what we discussed. It takes seven to ten days to open that doorway through which yesterday's shadows start seeping. Only then can you face your truth as to whether you are prepared to take this journey. If the client is not prepared at this time and calls to tell me this, then I feel pride, because he or she has been able to acknowledge his or her truth at that moment.

Once clients are truly ready, I start meeting with them once a week for approximately one hour. They begin to share some of their feelings, experiences, and thoughts, combined with a lot of tears and anger, but each time they come back, they have grown that much more within themselves. They have learned to love themselves more. They start to share how their sensory skills have begun to open, and how much lighter they feel about not carrying that burden inside.

I never point out directly if someone is not dealing with a specific issue. One of my helpers in the ethereal may telepathically make this statement, which I then pass on to the client. There's usually a reaction from the student that's with me, and then another doorway opens. It's a domino effect. When you open up about your truth and you share that moment in time with me, and you're telling me what you felt, what you're feeling at this moment, I may say something as simple as "and . . ." so that you have to finish the sentence. Recognize that you still have emotions about a situation, and are working towards your own truth. Some of the initial experiences with the ethereal could be connected to a past relative who was quite close to you. In one instance, a client came to me and said:

> CLIENT: When I was four, I lost my grandfather. And guess who I saw standing there when I was watching television the other day? My grandfather, just standing and smiling.
>
> JUDY: How did you feel about that experience?
>
> CLIENT: Really excited. It felt great to see him and know that life does go on.

The experience not only helps to remove some of the fear the client may have of those preconceived notions about the ethereal, it also affirms the existence of the ethereal world and makes the client hungrier to continue on this journey.

Once you've started opening to the visual aspects of the ethereal, then the other gifts that are infinite may start gradually showing themselves. But if you listen to your heart, you'll find yourself guided towards the gift that you're really comfortable with and work with that, and you'll go off on all kinds of journeys to use and expand on that particular gift. Examples of the types of gifts include: clairvoyance (seeing ethereal beings), clairaudience (hearing ethereal beings), clairsentience (sensing the presence of beings), mediumship (channeling), finding lost articles, and communicating with animals.

Once you begin to embrace your limitless gifts from the Creator, you have to open your mind to them and not let fear analyze and break them down. As we're walking in this world, we have to choose if we want to stay in this oblivious state or grow. When you start making these steps, the journey can be a very long and painful one. The people beside you become your judge and jury. They try to crush you and take control of your spirit because you can experience unconditional love. The adage "misery loves company" fits well here.

Once you've hit that truth, and you have found faith in yourself and faith in the Creator (as you see the Creator), that bond becomes invincible. The challenges in this world continue, but that bond remains. The doorways between you and the ethereal open one after another, one step after another. Only then can you say you truly understand unconditional love in its purest form.

If I had to try to describe what I'm like as a person when it comes to emotions, I would have to say that I do not live in "half-measures." There are no shades of gray when it comes to my thoughts and emotions. When you open up to the ethereal, the intensity of your emotions becomes quite high. If I watch a movie and I get caught up in it — *E.T. The Extra-Terrestrial* for example — it will take me several hours to come back down to a normal level of feeling. Every time I watch that movie, it's like watching it for the first time all over again. If anything makes me cry, I could end up sobbing for hours. You have to be willing to take the risk.

You may begin to have very vivid dreams in the first few

weeks. I suggest that you keep a journal of those dreams. In addition, get a small tape recorder and keep it with you on your desk at work, beside your bed, in your purse or briefcase. . . . At any given time you could have a fleeting thought or insight. Several days later you can listen to the tape and you may actually be able to validate some of the things you've written in your journal.

The energy work begins the minute that you start on your journey. Every emotion that you release, every truth that you face — that's energy. It's a purification of who you are. Then the documentation begins, and you become more aware — your sensory skills become more and more attuned. The ethereal sensory skill begins to show itself fleetingly. You've recognized the energy, the purification of self that you have taken on, and the heights that you have reached within yourself.

Once you start to feel the energy, you have a new sense of awareness and sensitivity that you can't explain. You could be walking to a corner store to pick up some milk. There are two or three people in the store along with you. You find your eyes suddenly turn towards one of them and you're hit with a strange feeling. Perhaps it's sadness, or perhaps it's joy. You may not be able to identify what it is you're feeling right then, but you know there is something that you are picking up. That awareness is not a bad thing, but rather the point where you decide, either consciously or subconsciously, whether or not you want to go further.

Once you've recognized the energy, then you may start receiving telepathic messages from the ethereal. Begin to experience those telepathic messages and allow the flashes —

the movie slides — to appear. You will begin to hear words of wisdom that seem to come out of nowhere, which help you on your daily journey in this world. You will identify certain connections in the spirit world that are very personal to you, and you will have gone beyond the preconditioned fear of all the horror stories that have influenced your thinking regarding the paranormal.

When you reach the step of forgiveness, you can begin to explore the energy even further, because you become more attuned to your inner self. If I'm not sending a client to a professional, I'll often suggest that they take Reiki. Reiki means "Universal Energy." It is a hands-on or distance healing practice using energy to heal on a physical, emotional, mental, and spiritual plane. It allows people to explore the concept of energy. When you begin to work with the ethereal, the energy levels rise to a higher vibration. I have a microphone in my reading room, and sometimes the energy gets to such a high vibration that the microphone just dies, or the tape recorder starts to break down. Learning to work with energy is one of the first things I teach my students.

Patience is the most difficult because once this begins, you still have to remain in no-time. I may then see a student every month at this point. Because there comes a time when these doorways open, the responsibility for the continuity of the gifts falls on the client. Once a student feels he or she has gotten as far as desired, then I may take on another student, but I have yet to see where it hasn't taken several years for a student to go from A to B. After all, my own journey didn't happen overnight.

It's important to note that while you're going through this learning, there will be times when you will challenge it. You'll probably have arguments with your Creator, and that's a good thing. Because if you don't question, and you don't challenge, you're being robotic. You're not being whole in body, mind, and spirit.

This dimension is full of the unexplained. There are teachers who have walked before us in this world and have left many lessons behind for us to call upon, and there are those who walk amongst us on a daily basis that we either recognize or don't recognize. There are healers, angelic beings, and prophets from many worlds whose only mission is to assist us in all manners possible without infringing on our free will so that we may attain the connection of unconditional love, peace, and harmony with all that we are, and all that is the Creator.

We are all attuned with the ethereal world. Once you've moved through your lessons then a new sensitivity develops, no matter who you are. Even though you may never associate it with the ethereal world, you do become consciously aware of this new sense. And that is the first step to attain before you can let these gifts grow to become positive, useful tools in your life. Once at that stage, you are able to move beyond feeling sorry for someone and shift to true empathy. You can get to the point where you have the ability to truly feel what this person feels: pain they may have suffered, or happiness they may have experienced.

Over the many years that I have been working with the ethereal, the one thing that I became very aware of is that people truly want a sense of knowing and of peace within themselves along with that connection to the ethereal and the Creator. The learning continues for all of us. The key thing is, even though you've got so many years of preconditioning to release and the world around you is full of fear and doubts and questions, once you've gone through the exercises and reached that state, fear can no longer control you. You have that extra edge where you can be in control, acting on free will. If that moment of fear or panic starts to appear, almost simultaneously you can shift to:

> CLIENT: Okay . . . what's the real message here? Why am I reacting this way?

All of a sudden there's a sense of calm inside of you. If you can reach that first stage and open up the doorway, you can immediately begin to shift into a new plane where understanding and self-love are prominent. If you hit a spot where you're going through a challenge to get into that place, I always tell those that I work with:

> JUDY: Okay, if you're going through a bit of a tug-of-war and you're not getting a handle on the lesson in the situation as quickly as you'd like, then do something to totally pull you away from that situation. Go to a show. Go for a walk. Put music on as loud as you want. Watch a silly sitcom. Do anything to totally distract you from it. So when you do go back and begin to reflect again, remember that you are in control of who you are.
> Fear is then in the shadows and you can continue with your internal work.

It's important to recognize that whatever your walk in life is, whatever your journey is, honor yourself by knowing that all you are in this world — the role you play, the interactions you have with others — is all a gift. Your life has been a contribution and should be honored by yourself and others.

EXERCISE:

Be aware of all the energy around you. With no expectancies, walk through your home in a totally relaxed state of mind and body. Hold your hand slightly over something, such as a stone. Close your eyes, breathe deeply, and allow yourself to tune in and feel the energy of that object. It may be a sense of coolness that you feel. It may be a sense of pressure. Each individual might experience a different sensation, but the important thing to note is that you have felt a form of energy. Next, move to a plant and go through the same process. You may feel warmth this time, a pulsation, but note the distinct differences in the energies. Hold your hand over something that you treasure with a sense of love, such as a picture or a locket, and you may feel a tingling in your fingers, or an overwhelming sense of warmth. Recognize, once again, the different energies. You can carry this exercise out of your personal domain as well. Learn to feel the energy of a tree, an animal, an elder, a child, and train yourself to tune into the energy and hear your spirit within guiding you to what you should know about the energy you have captured.

The Opposite of Fear

Now the tree is a full-fledged oak, having distributed its own acorns and weathered the storms. It has collected many lessons and released some as well. From age forty to infinity, the focus switches. As they grow older, people begin to question what their greater soul purpose is, and long to reclaim their spirit.

One thing that is important to recognize while on your healing journey is that you can backslide at any time. The moment you surrender to fear, you're done for that period of time, until once again you return to facing your truth and acknowledging the experiences. For as long as you are part of this world, that little fearmonger will pop up every once in a while. But with the wisdom that comes from all these lessons, you learn to recognize it instantly. Once you recognize fear, then you can change the pattern. The opposite of fear is love. That stepping stone from fear to love is truth. The truth comes when we forgive, starting with ourselves.

Sometimes, I sit back and say: "Thank you, Creator, for having such HUMUNGOUS unconditional love because you're held responsible for everything!"

After we're done blaming the Creator, then we hold

everybody else responsible. Then we turn around and hold the abstract responsible. What I really hope for mankind is that one day people will quit holding everyone else responsible and reach a point where they say: "I've made all these choices either consciously or subconsciously. What is my learning and how can I learn to love myself unconditionally?"

The process begins with looking at your yesterdays and forgiving the past. I went through a whole gamut of experiences. I allowed them to happen to me. I see the wisdom now, but I didn't see it then. As a child, if I had known this program that had been pre-written, it would have removed my freedom of choice and I am grateful that I did not lose that.

After losing the restaurant, RJ started driving a semi. Vivian had moved out with her boyfriend after Rachel's birthday. I was unemployed, unable to get any readings. Even if people had wanted me to read, I just couldn't. The situation was desperate for all of us. So I decided to travel with RJ and Rachel in the semi for a couple of months in the hopes that we would actually start to put the pieces together and find somewhere to settle down. I took a leave of absence from school for Rachel for two or three months because, in my mind, she had been traumatized with all of these shifts and losses.

We moved to Burritt's Rapids in 1986. We found a home beside a little store and I was in seventh heaven. There were wildflowers growing in the backyard, which was in total disarray, and there was an old, decrepit tree. I figured we'd finally get our lives together. I knew that RJ was not drinking on the job. Living in Burritt's Rapids was a healing time. I started doing readings again, but there was still no price tag attached.

I was beginning to get comfortable in my skin once more.

In this open-concept house, which we were renting, there was an old country kitchen with a staircase that led to a second level. Right at the bottom of the stairs was a large window. On a Sunday morning in early summer, while RJ was home and his kids were visiting us for the weekend, I had an amazing experience. I came down the stairs at around seven and almost jumped out of my skin. There was a figure standing just outside the full-length window at the bottom of the stairs: another visitor.

This all happened in a very short space of time because RJ usually came down within five minutes after me. Now, this visitor had to be well over seven feet tall. His bare feet appeared to be about two inches off the ground and all he was wearing was a simple white gown. His sleeves were about two inches above the wrist. I remember his fingers being very long and thin. His dirty blond hair was brought back flat with finger waves, reminiscent of a 1920s style. He had a Grecian nose, and old, wise eyes, of the most beautiful shade of blue. He also had high cheekbones, very white skin, and lips that were in perfect proportion with his face. He wore a hint of a smile as he spoke to me telepathically, and I received the message that I should not be afraid. No matter what, things would eventually be all right. I was not to give up; I wasn't being deserted by my Maker. I had to know that and *believe* that. Then he levitated further and transformed into a hummingbird.

By then RJ was on his way down, with me yelling: "Did you see him? Did you see him?"

"See who? I didn't see anyone," RJ said.

I was so excited, I phoned my mother. It was the first time I told my mother about a visitor. I had never shared anything of that nature with her before.

"Mom, you won't believe it. I was visited by an angel."

"Are you sure? Are you sure you weren't just dreaming?" she asked.

"No. I know what I saw."

Then, I babbled on about my childhood experience with the visitor in my bedroom.

"You never told me that!" she said.

"No, but I'm telling you now."

The conversation wasn't terribly encouraging. Shortly after the phone call, the kids got up and things started going back to normal. The earlier scene was replaying itself in my mind and I was on a high. Then, all of a sudden I started to feel completely deflated.

"Maybe you just think you saw it, because you wish you had seen it," I kept thinking.

Then I thought, "No, you know you saw it. You know it took place. What are you doing, Judy? Don't do this to yourself."

This mental combat went on and off all day.

Finally, I said to my Maker: "He told me that You loved me, that everything was going to be all right and that I wasn't to be afraid. If this really happened, please let me know it happened."

I couldn't get the image of that visitor out of my mind. At suppertime, we decided to eat at the picnic table near the old, dead tree. Although RJ knew the visitor had been there, I hadn't told the kids. While we were sitting around the picnic table, all of a sudden RJ's eleven-year-old son, Michael, exclaimed: "Judy, look up!"

Perched on the tip of a low branch was a hummingbird. The hummingbird nodded three times and then flew away. In my mind I said, "Thank you thank you thank you . . . for letting me know."

I interpreted the message to mean that everything would be okay from that day forth. However . . . the people who owned the store ended up losing it, and had to move from their apartment above the store back into the house they owned: the house we were presently occupying. We had to give up our home in Burritt's Rapids, this beautiful home that I loved.

From there, we moved to North Augusta into another very old home. It was the early fall of 1986, and by then both RJ and I were trying to get a semblance of work together. One evening, after being away for the day, we came home to two private detectives. They informed us that RJ and I were being charged under the Nursing Home Act for pilfering of funds. We were brought in and fingerprinted. I couldn't understand how this had happened.

"Well what are they charging *me* for? I had nothing to do with this. I don't even know anything about the nursing home business," I said.

"Remember I told you my brother and my ex-partner had taken all the money out of the nursing home. The trust fund? I've been trying to pay it back ever since. All the money is back there. What they're doing is charging us because it had been used off and on," he told me.

When I had power of attorney and was moving funds from

one account to the other, I was actually breaking the law without realizing it. There was no money missing, but the act itself was illegal, and RJ took the blame. Consequently, we could no longer afford to live in our house in North Augusta, so we had to move into a cheaper home in Frankville. It was 1987. As soon as we moved to Frankville, the story hit the newspapers: NURSING HOME OWNER CHARGED WITH MISAPPROPRIATION OF FUNDS.

We ended up in court even though there was no money missing. They charged RJ under the Nursing Home Act and tried to make him plead guilty to a number of charges that essentially translated into theft. I was also being charged. At this point, I still loved RJ and as far as I knew from the stories he had told me, both his brothers had royally screwed him, as had his ex-wife and father. And yet, he would not accuse his brother or ex-partner.

"If you want," he said to me, "I'll plead guilty and they'll drop whatever charges are against you."

"You're asking me to let you plead guilty to something that, based on what you've told me, you did not do. I can't let you plead guilty just for my sake. I couldn't live with myself, regardless of the consequences," I told him.

So the decision was made. We would plead not guilty.

While I endured many things, I also received ethereal protection, and a perfect instance of this occurred around the time we were dealing with the legal situation. Vivian was living with her boyfriend at the time, but Rachel was still with me. We all decided to go to a cattle sale barn one night. Vivian left with her boyfriend and Rachel in one car, RJ and I were in the other. There was only one highway we could follow to get to the sale barn, and we left about ten minutes after Vivian. While they were driving, an older woman cut them off just outside of Smith's Falls, and to avoid hitting another car head on, they swung into a driveway and hit a large tree.

RJ and I would have had no choice but to drive by that accident scene. When there is an accident, the police block off the area and wave people by. This highway was small. Passing an accident scene would be like looking across the street. I drove by that accident scene and *saw nothing*.

RJ and I arrived at the sale barn, but the kids weren't there. Meanwhile, Vivian had told the police where to find us. RJ and I walked around the sale barn. I even saw uniformed policemen. They had a description of us, but they didn't find us, and there weren't that many people there at the time.

They paged us at the barn; we didn't hear it. We called to see if they returned home; there was no answer. When I hung up the phone, I suddenly became very agitated. I remember telling RJ, "There's something terribly wrong. I can feel it. I want to go home NOW."

I have to give RJ credit; if ever, out of the blue, I became absolutely agitated, he would not question me.

"Fine, we'll go home," he said.

We passed the ambulance, and the accident scene — the vehicle was still there, it hadn't been towed — but we *still* didn't see it. We got home, walked into the house, and I repeated, "There's something wrong with the kids."

Immediately, the phone rang. It was Vivian's boyfriend's father.

"I'm at the hospital, Judy. The kids were in an accident."

"I'm on my way," I said.

"No no, everything's fine."

"I'm on my way."

I hung up the phone. Now, what normally would have been a twenty-minute journey took under ten minutes. I arrived at the hospital and discovered that while Rachel had been hurt, Vivian was in worse shape. The doctors could tell there was something terribly wrong with Vivian because of her white blood cell count, but the X-rays didn't reveal anything. She was lying in a gurney when I told her to get out of bed. All I kept seeing was a division: a slice.

"Get out of bed," I repeated.

"I can't. I'm in so much pain."

I said, "You're going to get out of the bed!" So I helped her get up, and as soon as she managed to stand, she said, "Mom, I can't! I'm in too much pain."

I laid her back down and turned to the doctor.

"Now take an X-ray, you'll see it."

The seatbelt had severed her intestine, but the cut was so clean, it was undetectable. Because I had insisted that she get out of bed, the intestine had moved. They took an X-ray and saw it right away. Vivian was rushed into emergency surgery. All the while, I contained my emotions. Four hours later she was still in surgery. When the doctor, our family physician, came out of the emergency room, I was leaning against the wall. He came towards me.

"It's fine," he said. "We had to give her a temporary colostomy and take a little piece of the bowel out because of the damage, but she'll be fine."

Suddenly, I felt a silent scream coming. The doctor just held me against the wall as this silent scream erupted from me. By the time I was finished, I could feel myself needing to collapse. He helped me into the visitor's room.

"Are you going to be all right? Do you want me to give you something?"

"No," I said.

"It will be a half an hour before you can see her," he told me.

By then, I had gained some control again. I saw my daughter and knew she was going to be all right. Later, Vivian told me that she had dreamt about the accident two weeks prior. She knew that Rachel would be in the vehicle and that she would be the one who was hurt the most. The ethereal had come to protect me from seeing my children at the side of the road. I know I would not have been able to handle that situation the same way if we had not been veiled.

A friend of mine had a similar experience. She was unpacking her car, moving her nineteen-year-old son into his apartment, when she realized he had collapsed on the side of the road. He was having a seizure. A woman who had lunched nearby knew exactly what to do. She had never eaten in that restaurant before, and couldn't understand why she felt drawn to do so until after helping the young man. The ambulance that arrived was instructed to take him to the first available hospital, which turned out to be affiliated with one of the top neurological hospitals on the continent. The joint rooms were all occupied with women, so he was assigned a private room, which allowed for his family to stay with him overnight. Since surgery, he has had the occasional seizure, and in all cases it has happened in a safe environment where there was either a friend or, in one case, a nurse he knew there to help. While his experience was extreme, the ethereal was there, setting up the situation so that he was protected as much as possible. The ethereal is always there to protect us, even when we feel at our lowest. Sometimes it's a challenge to acknowledge, but we are never alone.

The nursing home situation was certainly a low point. The media exposure and local newspaper stories were continuous. Rachel was sixteen at the time, and it was very hard on her. There was such hate projected at us: we were judged and hung before the case even got to court. Also at that time, the government intended to make examples of all kinds of nursing homes and clean up the system, and we were part of that.

In court, RJ and I stood and pleaded not guilty. On a strong recommendation from our lawyer, we never took the stand on our behalf. The trial went on for about ten days. During the trial, the prosecution would uncover stuff unexpectedly that the defense knew nothing about. The prosecution even tried to bring up my gifts, but the judge said, "I don't want to hear about any of this hocus-pocus stuff."

They tried to bring up RJ's drinking, claiming that he was always under the influence of alcohol.

"Don't want to hear about that, either," the judge said.

At the end of the trial, it boiled down to two facts: there was no missing money, but under the Nursing Home Act, a criminal offense had been committed. RJ was sentenced to eighteen months in prison. I was sentenced to a year's probation, which translated into one hundred hours of community service, a two-thousand-dollar fine, and because they couldn't find receipts for two things, I had to pay an additional six hundred dollars. In the end, after everything we endured in court, I received a full pardon in 1998 and RJ received one in 2001.

At that time, however, I was a destitute woman with a sixteen-year-old daughter, living in a small community in the public eye. I had a husband who was going to jail for something he didn't do, and I still believed all this time that he didn't do it. Who was going to hire me?

Every visiting day, I would bring the children to see RJ in the minimum security prison. Whenever a few people called me up to do readings, I would do them. It was the dead of winter, and I was living in a farmhouse with Rachel with next to nothing to eat. Several times, food was delivered to the house and I found out a couple of years later that my first husband, Ivan, had arranged for it. He had discovered through the newspaper articles that I was destitute. Apparently, there was no way anyone could convince him that I had ever done anything to take money from the residents. He knew me well enough. So he had food brought to us, but I was never supposed to know it was from him. I believe it was his way of apologizing. I didn't question it; I was just too thankful.

I was on social assistance at this point and getting the bare minimum. By the time the rent was paid, and I had bought a few groceries, there was never enough money for the heat. I continued to pray for a miracle, even though I was angry. I wasn't looking for the lessons at that point.

"How can You let this happen? There's a child here, too.

Why did You let me do this to myself?" I asked my Maker.

About a week prior, I had called to see if I could get some oil because we were so cold. I found out that without cash, it was impossible. One morning, when it was *really* cold and I turned the stove burners on to try to heat up the kitchen, there was a knock on my door. The house we were living in was on an acre and a half of land with a long driveway leading to it, so you could see any car that was arriving or departing. I opened the door and a man was standing there: just an ordinary looking man who appeared to have a suit on under his coat.

"Are you Judy?" he asked.

"Yes, I am," I said.

"Here, I have something for you."

He handed me an envelope. I looked down at my hand, at the envelope, and by the time I looked up again, he was gone. I stuck my head out but I couldn't see a car. So I closed the door quickly to keep out the cold, opened the envelope, and inside was enough money to pay for a tank of oil. No note, no explanation. To this day I still have no idea where it came from, but I did remember to say thank you. We could now have heat in the house.

I called the welfare office and they sent me a social worker. He was a young pup, in his early twenties, but with total empathy in his eyes. He suggested I find a job.

"I'm relatively uneducated. What do you want me to do?"

"Have you ever thought about going to college?" he asked me.

"Why would I go to college? I can't afford that. How am I going to get gas for the car to go to college? The closest place is Brockville. I'd freeze up while writing an entrance exam. I'm not smart enough."

"How do you know you're not smart enough?" he asked.

"I've heard it all my life."

He said, "You really don't know how smart you are. Maybe it's time you find out. What would you like to do?"

"Exactly what you do," I said.

"You can, you know. Even with a criminal record," he told me. "Why don't you go down and find out what the courses are?"

"Are you going to take me there?" I asked.

"Yes, I'll drive you," he said. "Let's pick a date."

So, we picked a date and he took me to the college. I read the calendar description of what it took in order to become a Life Skills Coach. I liked everything that it said. It was a ten-month course about helping people adjust to life and deal with life's problems. I could apply as a mature student.

I said to myself, "Well, if I'm supposed to be so smart, I also want to be a teacher of adults." That was a two-year course. I gave myself less than a year to do all of this, if I was accepted. I also refused to write an entrance exam. When I spoke with the admission's office, I gave them my terms.

"I'm not writing an entrance exam. You can either let me take these courses without the exam, and let me fast-track and do them within the next ten months or I won't do it."

"You'll never be able to pull it off," they said.

"Watch me."

So the college agreed to give me a shot, but I had to find my own travel arrangements. I begged until somebody said:

"Yes, we'll give you a ride every day if you stick this out."

As for tuition fees, I honestly don't know where the money came from to pay for my course. It was possibly social services or an anonymous gift. To this day, I see it as divine intervention because I never had to worry about it.

In the meantime, Rachel had quit school and refused to go back. With all the hardships we'd been through, and the last bit of embarrassment in the community, she couldn't deal with it. I decided not to push her until I got my own life together.

The most difficult thing I found with college was the battle within. I did not lack intelligence. I *was* smart. I was capable of this. I would not fail, and that was a real struggle. Sitting down in a structured room in order to write an exam was one of the most horrifying experiences I'd ever had. I felt totally restricted, almost claustrophobic. I was able to identify the fear, however, and acknowledge it. I connected with my Creator and said, "Okay I've got to do this. Can you help me?" So, I approached the professor.

"Do you mind if I sit at that last seat by the door? When it comes to sitting in a closed room with the door shut and having to write an exam . . ."

Being near that door would give me a sense of relief, that any given time I could just walk out. I had owned up to that truth, accepted it, and found the courage to tell my professor about it, and because of that, I was allotted that seat.

At the end of the course, I was told that I had passed the exams. So, in 1988, after ten months of school, I graduated with distinction and honors in both adult education and life skills coaching, receiving two diplomas.

A few months before RJ was to be released from prison, and before my graduation, I decided I couldn't let our marriage continue. I had been doing a lot of soul searching and it was time to rebuild my life. While he was incarcerated, I started to find out some things about him I had not known. All those black coffees RJ had been drinking throughout the day — about fifteen cups — were actually Café Royales: rye and coffee. He had bottles of rye hidden in the retirement home. So the man that I married was not the man I thought he was.

When we don't want to see the reality we are living, it's common to put on those rose-colored glasses, a symptom of denial. It's easier to ignore the truth than to face it. "The situation is too complicated," "It's not so bad," "Things will change" — all of these excuses come out and every one is fear-based. Fear of change, fear of being alone, or fear of failure, to name a few. It can be a deadly cycle, constantly making us surrender to the situation and keeping us from moving forward. Yet, the only one preventing you from moving forward is *you*. You hold the power.

"That's it," I finally said. "I know I'm not stupid. I can start my life over. I'm not taking this man back. It's done. This marriage is done."

My decision came close to his release date. When you're released, you're still on parole for a short period of time until you've served the remainder of your sentence. He had spent one year in jail. Now that I had made the decision to end the marriage, RJ had to find another place to live. Whoever was picking him up would have to supply the prison with a driver's license number and an address and phone number where RJ could be reached. That didn't stop me. I went to see him in prison that day and I told him it was over.

A week later, a friend of ours showed up. Later, I always questioned if RJ had talked to this friend about the fact that I had asked for a divorce because he said, "You can't do this. You can't kick a dog when he's down. He's had all this shit put on him."

He went on and on, laying on the guilt and talking about responsibility.

"Okay," I said, finally. "I'll let him come back home." So I went next visiting day to see him and told him of my decision. I supplied the driver's license and necessary information. The day before I brought him back to the house, I was filled with fury: at the situation, at RJ, and at myself. Poor Rachel barricaded herself in her bedroom because I lost it, breaking down and screaming while beating the top of my stove with a cast-iron pot. I literally bent the pot in half.

I picked RJ up early in the morning and he came back to the house. Shortly thereafter, we moved to Arnprior, Ontario. It was 1989 and I still believed we had a chance to rebuild our life, even after all the traumas we had lived through. I was working with developmentally and physically handicapped individuals using the skills I learned at college. Plus, I was doing readings. People continued to call and the crowd was getting bigger. I was still only spending ten to fifteen minutes reading each person. RJ had returned to trucking, and we were going to get our act together. We were going to make it work.

We soon had the opportunity to rent a trailer in Delta with

the idea that we could eventually own this mobile home, so we went for it. Vivian's common-law husband had been laid off and they couldn't afford their own apartment, so they moved into the trailer with us.

"Don't worry, we'll make it," I told her. It had become my philosophy. "No matter what, we'll make it."

At the point when I started working with Brenda, I had gone beyond right or wrong in life and saw each experience as a tool. It wasn't as though Brenda gave me some validation with regards to my gifts, but she helped me feel comfortable in my own skin with my own philosophies. I could feel a real vicious anger building up inside of me and I had to come to terms with the fact that there was nothing that I could do to make my husband change his perspective. We all have a tendency to try to mold people to what we think would be better. That was an important lesson for me to learn. The funny thing is, today I see everything RJ did in a positive light, no matter how ugly it had been at the time.

When I began seeing Brenda, I had to face the truth of how much anger I really felt from the issues that had taken place in both my marriages. What Brenda did was help me walk, not run, through each issue. Even if I sat for moments of silence where I had to face a certain feeling or emotion, until I was really ready to look at the situation, there was no pressure to speak.

During my sessions with her, I shocked myself with some of the emotions that I was experiencing. Once I recognized them, Brenda got me to express them until they surfaced and faded. Imagine looking out in the distance and seeing this twister beginning, then coming closer until it becomes a full tornado. When that happens, it's difficult to ignore. But once that tornado comes forth, you have the choice of whether or not you are ready to release it. If you want to get rid of it, what can you do? You have to find a way to accept that the tornado exists, then deal with it in order to make it go away.

On more than one occasion, I said: "I don't want to deal with this right now."

Brenda would reply: "That's fine. You're obviously not ready."

Remember, this is *your* journey.

My mother used to be able to control and manipulate me emotionally because I thrived for the day when I would hear her say: "Judy. I love you. I always have loved you. You were a great child and a blessing to me." Then I came to terms with the fact that we are not responsible for the steps of growth that other people take. To this day, I still don't always like my mother's behavior, but now I can separate the behavior from the person and I've learned to say thank you: "Thank you for the reminder to continue to pray for my mother so that hopefully, before she leaves this planet, knowledge and wisdom will grow inside of her so she can understand unconditional love."

A few weeks before working on this book, I took my mother out for brunch. A week prior to meeting her, I felt afraid about telling her my writing plans. I thought, "I can't share it, I can't tell her. All hell will break loose." It took me a couple of days of thought and prayer until I turned around and said: "What are you doing? You know better than this!"

So halfway through brunch I said, "By the way, Mom, I'm writing a book."

"What kind of book?" she inquired.

"It's going to be about who I am and my life experiences from my early childhood on."

I never got further than that. My mother went ballistic. She kept bringing up past incidents, and I let her finish.

"Now, Mom," I said. "You had your say. I'm going to tell you something. The only perspective I can speak from is my own. I know I'm not mentally incapacitated because I dealt with enough psychologists and psychiatrists to realize that. When I speak of my truth and my experiences, I speak of them as I remember them. There's no right or wrong here and I want you to know that. So let's agree to disagree. You have your way of looking at it and I have mine. I truly believe that children are products of their environment as they're growing up. If you look at the alcoholism and abuse surrounding your six children you'll see perfect examples of that. But, I also believe, Mom, that you reach a point in adulthood where you can no longer use that as a crutch. I'll use me as an example. Let's say I was an alcoholic. I have to stop saying 'I'm an alcoholic today because my mother was an alcoholic.' The same way my children can't say they're behaving in a certain fashion today because they saw me behaving in a certain fashion. There comes a time when I have to own up to my actions and recognize that maybe I put myself in that scenario by choice. You are an adult and now you must take responsibility for your choices. I've taken responsibility for mine. You now know I'm doing this book so let's move on to another topic."

And I switched the topic. I have to tell you there was a time when I could never have done that with my mother. I used to be petrified of anger. Now, I have seen how I was gifted from that experience. I am now able to see other people's unresolved anger. Knowing that allows me to help them, should they be ready to acknowledge it.

One of the things I learned with RJ was the importance of standing behind my convictions and recognizing and accepting that each individual must journey how they choose and in the time that they choose. My time with him reinforced my goal of self-love by recognizing what I could and could not live with. He taught me how to set goals for myself, and to work towards them both in the physical and the spiritual realms. He taught me how anger and hatred does not poison the one you direct it at, but poisons yourself.

My kids awakened the innocence of my inner child and the need for me to revisit that child and to honor her. They taught me to acknowledge my weaknesses in my parenting skills and the determination to learn and enhance them so that my children and grandchildren could benefit from them. They also taught me unconditional love and forgiveness, and gave me the strength to stand by what I believe in.

If you're greatly disturbed by a lot of past ghosts, find yourself the right counselor. Then, if you want to move to the ethereal level, I would suggest that you find a Reiki master that exhibits those very same qualities. This person can help you start to open up the door to do energy work, until you can eventually find a teacher that you're comfortable with to explore one-on-one work in order to grow and expand the ethereal connection, and experience unconditional love.

EXERCISE:

I will often ask clients if they have created a special area in their home that they can call their own — a serenity area where you can go and just "be." I recommend that in this area you play soft music, if you enjoy music, or burn a candle, put a plant nearby, and perhaps a small fountain. By doing this, you are bringing the elements of the world into this serenity place. Once there, allow yourself to drift, to read, to do whatever brings a peace and calm within the very core of your being, however briefly. That time allows you to honor yourself, and connect with the Creator. You will find that after trudging through the necessities of functioning in this world, and even dealing with the uglies, your stress will disappear. It is a perfect place to stop and acknowledge what you are feeling. Do you have a space you can call your own? Is there a way to create one for yourself? If not, then find a space externally that brings you peace and make the effort to go to that space at least once a week in order to be at one with yourself and connect with your spirit.

Truth, Trust, and Time

In early 1991, while working as a bartender at the Legion, I wrote this journal entry:

- ❀ I will save all my tips in a separate area, to do something for me.
- ❀ Have my own private bank account.
- ❀ Be free from personal debts.
- ❀ Live in an accommodation that can be afforded and be happy with the place.
- ❀ Have my days and nights busy doing something that I enjoy and work at a job I'm centered at, where I have a sense of purpose and completeness.
- ❀ Not be lonely anymore. Four years is enough.
- ❀ Learn to laugh and enjoy life again.
- ❀ Learn to love myself and learn to be selfish about some of my needs and wants.
- ❀ Chase my dreams, and to hell with all those who object.
- ❀ Be in good health both physically and mentally.
- ❀ Plan and save enough to go on a ten- to fourteen-day holiday by this time next year.
- ❀ Have enough to be self-sufficient.

- Sing, dance, and be merry as often as possible. To hell with the consequences.
- To accomplish all my goals.

I still had a long, tough road to travel before these could become a reality. Although I did accomplish many of them, the journey is not over.

I started using the term "Truth, Trust, and Time" — the three T's. I find that a lot of people have difficulty with those three factors, but they are needed in order to understand how to walk in the ethereal world if you choose to let it play a role in your life.

Truth: The truth begins with yourself. It comes from your spirit. But first, you must forgive yourself. This brings about unconditional love.

Trust: Trust involves learning to have faith in what your spirit is telling you. Trust what you're hearing and what you're feeling. Trust your heart, your spirit. It's the only thing in this world that will never lie to you.

Time: Everybody wants everything to happen *yesterday*. Everybody's working nine to five to put bread on the table. If you can, remove your watch on the weekend, and put it away. Let everything work out according to the natural course of time for a change and see how things move at that pace. It will take you a while to adjust, but you'll learn to recognize the time on a subconscious level, to the point where eventually you won't need a watch. You *trust* that things will take care of themselves because you've opened the ethereal window. Once again, you're back to freedom of choice. It's up to you whether or not you want to work with the three T's. However, if truth, trust, and time are not in your life, you can't move forward. You're stuck on this plane. It's like being stuck in a time warp.

Speaking of time warps, if you ever go through one, you'll be totally amazed. A year and a half ago, I drove from Carleton Place to Ottawa with two other people to do a group reading. While we were there, the experience with the visitors from the spirit world and the people in the room was very intense. The house we were working at was in the east end of Ottawa. It would take approximately forty-five minutes to get back to my home in Carleton Place. As we prepared to leave after the reading, I asked about the time as I had no idea how long we had been there. From the doorway where the three of us were standing, we could see the kitchen clock on the wall, which clearly indicated five minutes to ten. Margaret, the woman who was driving, and her sister also looked at their watches. She said: "Yes, it is five to ten and it is time to head back." So we left. The next morning I phoned Margaret.

"What do you think happened last night?" was how I started the conversation.

"I was wondering if you would call me, because my sister called me. The uncanny thing is, we were both in bed, in our nightgowns, when we looked at our clocks. They said five past ten."

We had actually gone through a time warp. Only ten minutes had passed from standing at that door to being in our nightgowns and sitting in bed. Simultaneously, we were drawn to look at the clock when we were in bed. Both women said that they felt completely refreshed in that period of time, which logically should have been an hour and a half. Another example of truth, trust, and time. We knew it took place, and we didn't have to understand it. All over the world, scientists are doing studies of the ethereal, but nobody has yet to come up with any kind of definite proof to explain it.

It's important to note the subtle messages from the ethereal world, like smelling intense perfume in an empty room, for example, or feeling the compulsion to share an idea, or sensing a loved one that has passed. Let's say you're going through a period of your life where there's a lot of stress. You may even feel desperation or depression. Suppose, also, that as a child you were very close to your grandmother. She was always a pillar of strength and wisdom to you. She may have passed on twenty years prior, but as you're standing in front of the mirror and brushing your hair, you sense a hand on your shoulder. Your thoughts then flash to your grandmother. Do not question the experience, but accept that yes, she is probably working as a guardian for you, reassuring you and letting you know that you're not alone. So your task is to note the subtle things and not ignore them, because there are no coincidences. There is a purpose for everything in life.

When you start to explore the three T's, the first thing you need to do is acknowledge your truth. Learn to respect and trust yourself, and allow yourself to go at your own pace. To get to that place of unconditional love, you need to respect that your journey takes time. When you begin your journey of truth, trust, and time, age is not an issue because the lessons that you have lived have given you a wisdom that can be the greatest gift.

The speed with which you move is dependant on how much you've experienced and what your life was like, among others. Everybody learns, grows, and heals at a different pace. You must trust that it will happen. And if you can walk with this, no matter how long it takes, you eventually will evolve to where you want to go.

When clients talk to me about a long-term relationship that has been falling apart, there is often a lot of anger and resentment, mostly towards themselves, because they're stuck in the situation. They're not listening to their truth, and consequently, they're not respecting themselves.

I can remember when Vivian was about thirty-one, she felt that her life wasn't coming together. She went from feeling completely deflated about it to deciding that she would not deal with it. She would not accept her gifts, even though they kept coming out in her dreams. Fighting who she was would not change things. I kept telling her:

JUDY: Until you come to terms with who you are and accept this, the patterns of your life will continue. I'm going to tell you right now you may as well not even worry about where your life is going, because you aren't going to find that perfect companion or have the family you want until you're thirty-five.

From then on, she would periodically ask:

VIVIAN: Well, what do you think? Is it going to happen soon?

JUDY: The more you worry about it, the more you're throwing that out into the universe and creating havoc

119

within yourself. You're on this Ferris wheel of worrying for nothing, feeling anxiety because something is not happening the way you want it. Just trust that it will happen, and stop worrying about when.

Sure enough, in the latter part of her thirty-fifth year, the right companion walked into her life. This gentleman already had a couple of children from a previous marriage, so Vivian was ecstatic to have a ready-made family. She also recently gave birth to a baby girl. Vivian did eventually find her soulmate, but she was not ready for it to happen until that time.

If you are strong with your gifts, it can be very difficult to have a relationship if your partner does not share your views. If you're interacting in a family situation where your partner uses the ethereal connection against you every time there's a conflict, it can be quite hurtful. In some cases, people associate walking in the ethereal with cultist concepts or heavy religion. There are still many misconceptions about spirituality versus structured religion. Both of them should be able to walk hand in hand without conflict, the same way homeopathy and Western medicine should be able to. In fact, we've reached a point where homeopathy and Western medicine are beginning to embrace each other. Spirituality and structured religion are *just* beginning to touch. People from both genders, every age group, and every sexual orientation are beginning to seek out knowledge of the ethereal plane. They want to know that connection, and now recognize that it is based on spirituality.

Write down your visions and your dreams until you are

able to differentiate between them. I also recommend that you don't try to analyze them right away, but set them aside for a day or two, then go back and try to see if you have any insight from what you've written. If you can't interpret the visions, then you should seek the knowledge of someone who is able to do this interpretation. Even if you do have insight into your visions, it's still a great idea to connect with somebody who has the ability to interpret some of them for you. That way, you can correlate everything.

When you walk in this world, you gain learning material that can lead to true inner knowledge. You may suffer human limitations, and endure many hardships, but you can grow from those experiences. It's not an easy process. I have yet to see anybody with strong gifts who didn't end up going through some form of heavy-duty education. Many in the medical profession might propose that these visions of the ethereal are all triggered due to childhood trauma, which makes them appear invalid. Everyone has gifts and the ability to connect with the ethereal. It's just a matter of recognizing your truth, trusting your spirit, and allowing yourself the time to grow.

EXERCISE:

Once you open up to the ethereal, you become aware of the different energies. If you attend a social function, remember to acknowledge encounters with others. Heed what your spirit is telling you, for that is your truth. For example, should you be introduced to someone who is so callous or caught in fear, immediately acknowledge that truth within yourself and slip away from that energy as soon as possible. Call for protective reinforcements from the Creator so that the negative energy cannot touch you in any way. Surround yourself with people who bring positive energies to you, and in turn, share your positive energy with them. Being around positive people is healing for both you and them. Who are the positive people in your life? How do you feel after spending time with them versus spending time with individuals who aren't as positive on an energetic level? Start to acknowledge the energy, and by doing so you will prevent personal energy drainage.

Removing the Rose-Colored Glasses

The reason why you must learn to honor yourself is because it's the basis of learning what unconditional love translates into. Until you learn to do this, it is impossible for you to love someone else in that manner and it's impossible to recognize those who are trying to show you love. I will honor myself by walking away from a situation, or avoiding it if I feel over-tired or vulnerable. If I have any appointments booked and I'm not in a good space, I'll call and reschedule the meeting time. I have learned that it is okay for me to say: "Going into that atmosphere will only create more havoc in me and I don't need to go there right now. At a later day, when I feel better, I can deal with this."

It's important for you to be able to honor your own needs. By doing so, you can better support those around you. Give yourself permission to take time out regularly, not only when you need it. One place I go to is my serenity room. There is an altar that acknowledges Mother Earth and all the gifts that she gives us. The four corners are honored with moments of silent prayer to the Creator, all past masters, teachers and healers, all angelic and golden light beings. There is a water fountain decorated with two white doves that was gifted to me along with different mementos that were given to me as gifts of love. There are multi-faceted crystals and stones from around the world, and a pyramid over this altar, which signifies energy. On the window is a large dream-catcher with a bald eagle in the center. In the corner cabinet is a native vase holding bits of ribbon and papers from different gifts that I have received. I ask that this vase be filled with the energy of these representations of love.

Surround yourself with daily reminders of love. Find a place where you can sit by yourself or with someone, and just be. Put things in your home that bring comfort and peace, share space and time with those that empower you through wisdom, knowledge, and caring, and do the same for them. By acknowledging the limitations of being human, by forgiving your foibles, and by forgiving those of others, you honor yourself. You could also choose a career that gives you a sense of wholeness and purpose, take time to walk and enjoy nature, decorate your home with colors, plants, and furnishings that give you a sense of warmth, or take time to enjoy lunch with a friend and share thoughts and feelings. Take time to cry. Learn how to laugh. Respect your physical body. Reach out and touch someone. Set no boundaries in experiencing, nurturing, caring, and sharing. Learn not to go into self-disgust when you believe you have made a mistake. Honor that, and see the lesson.

It took some time for me to learn the importance of honoring myself. I started to see some of my life patterns in my daughter Vivian and her common-law husband when they moved into the trailer with us. Around this time, she gave birth to a beautiful boy named Tommy. I was in the operating room when she went through her C-section, and was the first one to hold my grandson.

One evening, she and I went out to the bingo parlor. In the middle of playing bingo, I was struck with an insight. Out of the blue, I said:

"My God, check your bank account. He stole your money."

"Who stole my money? What are you talking about?" Vivian asked.

Vivian was working as a health care aide, and had a separate bank account from her spouse.

"I'm telling you, we have to go check your bank account."

"Settle down, Mom," she kept saying. "Where do you think that's coming from?"

"I'm not sure, I just know it."

We made our way to the bank so she could check her account. All the money was gone. There had been close to one thousand dollars in her account, and it was every cent she had. We drove home, and Vivian was fuming. She had started to realize that he was following the same pattern as RJ with regards to alcohol. When we got back to the trailer, she marched to the spot where she kept her bank card. It was still there. Then I saw a light go on in her eyes. She approached the area where she kept her checkbooks. There were checks missing.

Then she said to me, "Mom, I'm scared."

She admitted that she felt her life was in danger if she tried to leave him. I was always protective of my children, but now Tommy was part of the equation. There's nothing worse than an enraged grandmother.

When he came in, Vivian confronted him about the missing money. The two of them argued in the bedroom. Finally, she told him to get out.

He took a step towards her, then I said, "This is *my* home. You get out now or I'll call the police."

So he went outside and sat at the picnic table on the lawn.

"Mom," Vivian said. "We can't stay here and RJ's not due home until nine. He won't do anything with RJ here. I want him gone."

"Okay," I said. "Let's get in the car and get out of here. Put some stuff together for Tommy. We'll just go away for three or four hours until we know RJ's home."

When I got outside, Vivian's husband stood up from the picnic table. I walked towards him. Vivian and Tommy went straight for the car.

"This is as far as you go," I told him. "If you think you scare me because you're six-foot-something, you don't. I've had the toughest in my life. I'm telling you right now, I'm going to the store and I'm going to be gone twenty minutes. When I come back you'd better be gone. As far as your clothes, I'll have them put in a garbage bag and dropped off at your mother's home. If you're not gone, I'll press charges."

I got in the car with Vivian, and we drove away. She asked me to stop at a nearby store.

"I want to buy myself a pack of cigarettes," she said, shaking like a leaf. When she came out of the store, there was a problem.

"Mom, this guy's got a check that bounced, supposedly signed by me."

That was the first one.

"We better start looking around," I said.

Next, we went to the beer store. Sure enough, it was the same deal. The liquor store, too. We kept finding forged checks. Vivian paid every one of those bills. She explained the situation to each store owner, promising that she would take care of it. She consulted a lawyer, who said she could have her husband thrown in jail, but she decided against that course of action. Vivian did, however, get sole custody of Tommy. The last time her husband saw his son, Tommy was ten months old.

Facing those truths is empowering. It's like fine tuning a television set in order to get a better reception — there's more clarity in the picture, and the sound quality is better. In this world, there's never a break from dealing with all of your truths, except when you decide not to learn anymore. And when you decide to do that, then you go through some of the experiences I have!

You have choices. Vivian made a choice that night, to take her power back. She did not hide behind alcohol or drugs, or give up on living, but took a stand, which took courage. Don't be afraid to lean on those people close to you and ask for help. When you deal with reality, you evolve. You'll notice there is more clarity in your life, even in the moments when you're dealing with different individuals that cross your path. You reclaim your power when you honor yourself by standing up and saying: "No. I won't accept this."

We ended up moving back to Carleton Place in 1993, and I had come to the realization that I was not following my truth. So I went into a serious prayer session with my Maker.

"Okay," I said. "No matter what career I've tried my hand at, I am always doing these readings. If this is supposed to be my career, You'd better start hitting me with a sledgehammer because I'm not getting the message. If You want me to do this, then I have to find a way to get people to come. I haven't a clue what I'm supposed to charge them. So I tell You what I'm going to do. I'm going to put something together to advertise."

Now, there were rows upon rows of books in our apartment. I approached one of the shelves.

"I know those bibles are in here," I said. "I've got the King James version, the Roman Catholic bible, a Mormon bible. . . . You name it, I've got it. So, I'm going to close my eyes and I'm going to spin a half dozen times as fast as I can, and whatever bible I'm supposed to have, that's the one my hands will land on. I have to have some kind of reference that my gifts are linked with You. They can only be through You."

I spun, stumbled, put one hand on the shelf, pulled, then stumbled back to the nearest chair and sat for about twenty minutes until the nausea passed, as I suffer from motion sickness. When I was finally settled, I looked at what I had picked: the Roman Catholic bible.

"Great," I said. "Have me pick the one that's been my cross all my life!"

I believe God has a sense of humor. We humans sure put ourselves through trials; He's got to laugh at some of our foibles.

"Okay," I said. "I really don't know where to look in here. I want to get the right message if I'm going to try to put some kind of flyer together. I can tell You one thing, there will be angels on it."

I've always been partial to angels.

"It's not going to say 'psychic' on it because I don't like that word. So please help me put this together. I'm going to throw this bible up into the air, and let it open where it's supposed to. Then I'm going to spin again with my eyes closed and point down, and wherever my finger points, that sentence or phrase will become the heading of the flyer."

I threw the bible into the air, let it fall, all the while spinning around like crazy with my eyes closed. Weaving back and forth, I put my finger on something, then staggered to the chair and sat down while keeping my finger on this book. Another twenty minutes of recovery time and then I looked down at the bible. What you see at the top of my flyer is what was under my finger.

1 Corinthians 12,4: "There are different kinds of spiritual gifts, but the same spirit gives them all."

After I half-sketched the angels, I still had no title for the flyer I was designing. It was a Sunday morning when I said, "Okay, I've got all the angels. What should my flyer say?"

Then I felt the urge to write. It took me ten minutes to write down everything that is in my flyer.

"Well," I said after, "I guess this is Your way of telling me that it's the way it should be. So now when somebody shows up at the house, I'll give them a flyer."

There were already people calling me through word of mouth. I couldn't depend on RJ's paycheck to cover all of our bills, so the plan was to use a section of my bedroom as an office. I gave my flyer to someone to type up, then went to a printing shop. When I was told how much it would cost, there was a problem. I couldn't afford it.

"Let me think about it," I said. "I'll get back to you."

I told someone I knew that I had put a flyer together about myself and what I do, and that I was looking to have them printed.

"Why don't you go to this print shop?" she suggested. "They've just started up. They'll give you a break."

So I went to the new store, and the price was less than half of what the other shop was charging.

"I must really be supposed to do this," I thought.

Once the flyers were complete, I said to my Maker, "Okay, now for the last step. You let me know what price tag to put on these readings. I have no idea what I'm supposed to charge. You'll have to tell me. At the same time, I'm going to keep the barter system. I want to have that in case somebody's really stuck."

I already knew at this point that my gifts didn't work when it came to gaining insight on anything involving myself. A couple of days went by, then I received a phone call from a man who had heard about me through a friend and wanted to arrange an appointment. When he showed up, he never asked me how much I charged, and I never volunteered it. I spent about twenty-five minutes giving him a reading. When he left, he said: "I hope this will do," and handed me a sealed envelope.

"Thank you very much," I replied.

Before he left, I handed him a flyer. I didn't look in the envelope right away. I closed the door and walked up to the kitchen, plugged in the kettle, and then opened up the envelope, where I found a brand new fifty-dollar bill. And that's the price I've been charging ever since. I got a half dozen phone calls through that man. Soon, it got to the point where my phone was ringing constantly.

One of the women who came to see me was of native descent. She then recommended me to a native elder named Gordon. After I finished my session with him, I was drawn to ask him specific questions regarding native culture. His answers gave me a real sense of wonder.

"Hey," I thought to myself. "I think this is some of the stuff I'm supposed to be learning. I feel a sense of peace with this."

Almost immediately after he left, my visions grew more paramount. I noticed things were crossing my path in inexplicable ways. One of the first visions I had told me that I would be known as somebody that collects things and brings items together to return them to where they belong. That one really didn't make sense to me, but I recorded it anyhow. Then came Gordon's visit. Within a month or so of speaking to him, another individual connected with me to see if I would do a group reading for her. The first reading was in her antique store. She happened to be a collector of articles from the 1940s and '50s. After that session, she asked me to do another group reading at her home.

When I approached the house door, something kept pushing me back out. And the host, of course, was watching me. I went to take another step in, and this thing pushed me right back out the door.

"Is there a problem?" she asked.

"Well, yes. There is. There's something stopping me from

coming into your house. It's almost as if they want me to notice something."

"What could they want you to notice?"

"I don't know."

Then, I spoke to the entity. "Okay, I promise to look and see what it is. Will you let me in?"

I went to step forward again, and was allowed in, where I felt myself frozen in one spot. So I started scanning the room, and then I noticed a large artifact by the door. It seemed to have been carved out of a tree trunk, with a face on each side: one was smiling, one was angry. I recognized it as native and pointed to it.

"That . . . I'm not sure where it came from," the host said.

"Whatever it is, it's native," I explained.

"Well, I'm using it as a doorstop because it won't sell in the store. If you really like it, and want to have it, I promise to give it to you."

Instantly, I had this overwhelming sense of "yes!"

So I told her, "Yes, I do. I really would like it."

At that point, I was able to enter fully, and go through the evening. By the time I was finished, I was exhausted. RJ was picking me up because I wouldn't be able to drive for at least an hour after the session. I went to leave, not really thinking of grabbing the artifact. I stumbled slightly, and then got "*carving*."

"Were you serious about the carving?" I asked the host.

"Yes, it's yours. Here," she said as she handed it to me.

I had no idea what it represented. During the ride home, I had a sense of heaviness, almost a foreboding, that there was something I was supposed to do with the artifact. But I couldn't seem to tap into what, exactly. When we got back home, I brought it to the area that I had set up in my bedroom for readings, which consisted of two chairs and a table in front of a window. Sensing anxiety from it, I stood it behind the chair at the other end of the bedroom, where I couldn't see it.

Eventually, we went to bed. I was up all night because all I could hear was the sound of drums beating and a wailing chant. I woke up RJ once and asked him if he could hear anything.

"No. You're dreaming. Go back to sleep."

I got out of bed, and the closer I walked towards the carving, the louder and more overpowering the sound became. So I was really distressed and tired the next morning.

"Okay," I reasoned with my Creator. "This obviously means something. You've got to help me with this. I don't know what I'm supposed to do with the artifact. I don't even know what it is, but I don't like what I'm feeling and I'm so tired." Gordon, the native elder who had come for a reading, immediately crossed my mind. I wasn't sure how I was going to find this man, so I went through the scraps of paper on which I had written down the names of people who had made appointments, and I located his name and phone number. I called and connected with an answering machine, asking him to call me back, which he did within the hour.

"Do you remember who I am?" I asked.

"Yes, I do. I know exactly who you are."

I began to relay the story of going to the house, what had taken place, and how I ended up with the carving. He asked me to describe the artifact. I mentioned the coloring, the shapes of the mouths, the two faces, and other details. I told him what it did to keep me up at night. Gordon instructed me to cover it with a white sheet.

"Whatever you do, do not uncover it."

"Will that let me sleep?" I asked.

"It should let you sleep now that we've connected. I believe it was stolen from a native tribe. What I'll do now is find out if I'm right. And if I'm right, this artifact has been missing for many years.

It took him three days to get back to me. In the meantime, I covered it and talked to it.

"Now I'm doing the right thing, aren't I? It's in somebody else's court. Please let me sleep."

I did manage to sleep and read for my other clients without interruption. The night before Gordon called back, the drums and the chanting started again. I was up all night. There was a different tempo this time, almost an excited one.

The next morning, exhausted, I said, "I'll probably be hearing from Gordon."

Sure enough, the phone rang early that morning.

"I know what it is. It belongs to the Mohawk nation."

It was a ceremonial mask, which was agitated because it needed to be fed and used in ceremonies, but hadn't because it had been stolen so many years ago. Gordon told me that I was never to uncover it. He was going to receive instructions from an elder or a shaman from the Mohawk tribe and then he would pick it up and deliver it to them.

"I hope it doesn't take too long," I said. "I can't go on without much sleep."

The drum never kept me awake after that. About two weeks later, Gordon called back.

"I'll be there at ten tomorrow morning. I'm going to wrap it in red felt. It will be used in the tribe's strawberry festival so there'll be a full ceremony."

The piece was authenticated, and it was indeed a stolen Mohawk ceremonial artifact. Gordon thanked me, and the Mohawk tribe sent me a little box, which I appreciated. That was one instance where I understood what it meant to be a collector or gatherer, returning things to people. And there were several objects I found over the years. I continue to record my visions and interpret them. Sometimes I have my own insights but I also have friends and teachers who give me feedback.

In late 1994, I was doing a lot of readings and also appearing at many house parties. Business really avalanched. At that point, RJ approached me.

"You make more than enough money," RJ said. "And you make more money than I'll ever make. How about if I stay home and drive you to your appointments so you don't have to worry about it." I would always have to sit for an hour before I could even attempt to drive home. I needed that time to come back down to the earthly plane.

"I'll take care of paying the bills," he said. "I really will."

Well, we were surviving at least. He was never without his alcohol, but I was busy working, and as long as he stayed out of my way, I didn't care what he did.

The man who owned the apartment we were living in wanted to sell the building. He was also a real estate agent. He told us that he'd give us a great deal on a house. RJ convinced me, even though I didn't want to buy that house. I just didn't have it in me anymore to fight with this man. So we moved to a house in Carleton Place on December 1. RJ was going to take care of the finances, putting aside any extra money after the bills were paid. Within the first few months, we discovered that we had been deceived about the house. We didn't even own the land it was on.

"I told you I didn't want this house," I argued. "I want to get out of it. They can take it back as far as I'm concerned."

The situation became an ongoing legal battle. Rachel and her husband, whom she married earlier that year, had become unemployed with no place to live. Rachel was expecting their first child, and until they got themselves re-established, I had said that they could live in the basement, as long as they finished it off into an apartment. I still believed that once the court case was over, we were going to end up with this house. The problem is, it's usually the ones with the money and power that win. My kids were coming and going. RJ's nose was out of joint because there was a lock on the basement door and he felt he should be able to go in and out whenever he pleased. There were a lot of confrontations. I was trying to get through fifteen people a day to keep everybody supported. I had a responsibility to the children and grandchildren. Even though my children were adults, I wasn't going to leave them on the street.

Finally, I physically collapsed. I put my foot down.

"I'm getting an office. I'm moving out of the house to do my work. I can't function here. There is too much confusion and distraction at home."

My father was diagnosed with Alzheimer's in 1999, and spent ten months in a nursing home and hospital. Because I didn't have a chance to be really close to my father, I had long conversations with my Creator, asking Him: "When my father's time comes to pass, please let me be there."

Vivian spent many years working in nursing homes with the elderly, so she was very knowledgeable about how the system worked. When my father was put into the home, a home Vivian had once worked in, she told me what to expect.

"I'm going to tell you right now, he won't last very long. When it comes to drugs and so forth, they'll really pump them into him. They're going to start him on morphine the minute he isn't physically feeling well."

She told me exactly which nurse would be the one to initiate the morphine dosages and talk my mother into giving it to Dad. Vivian was able to disassociate herself somewhat from the situation because of her profession, even though she desperately loved her grandfather. A couple of days before he passed away, while he was unconscious, I would sit at the foot of his bed and watch him. I could actually see a mist covering him that would rise from his body, and go back in.

When the nurses told my mother it was time, we all received a call. The first people to arrive were my mother and me. I kept giving thanks for the opportunity to be with my father at this time. That was one of the greatest gifts my Maker could give me. I knew from what I had read and what my daughter had told me that the last thing to go was his hearing. An awful sound rattled from him, due to chest congestion from pneumonia. The moment he passed on, we walked into the room and I knew exactly what was happening. From my perspective, his eyes opened wide and that awful rattling stopped. He was looking upward. I put one hand on his, and put my other hand on top of his head.

"It's okay, Dad," I said. "Take God's hand. Go with Him, Dad."

All I heard was, "Ohhhhh."

The most peaceful look came over his face, as though he was experiencing total recognition.

"Remember Dad, I love you. I always have and all yesterdays are forgiven," I whispered when my mom ran out to get the nurse.

Through my hands I actually felt him leaving this body. I was in total awe and felt such a sense of peace. The nurse came in to confirm his death and she closed his eyes and adjusted the blankets. When we came back into the room about five minutes later, I asked my mother if I could have a lock of my father's hair. She consented, and also agreed to give me the only other thing I wanted of my father's: the rosary he had by his bed.

I went to work the next day because I had booked a client, but I was very much in thought. On the drive to work, I prayed to my Maker.

"Could You please let me know that my father has his wings?"

All of a sudden, RJ slammed on the brakes, snapping me out of my thoughts.

"What was going on?" I asked.

"I can't believe you didn't see that," he said.

"Well, I was in prayer. What?"

And he did a U-turn and drove about half a block.

"The car ahead of us hit a hawk," he said.

The hawk has very special significance for me. In native teachings, Hawk is the Messenger. So I got out of the car, broke a cigarette, spread tobacco around the hawk, and prayed. Then, I asked the Creator if I could have some of its feathers. Normally when you have a fresh kill, you can't pull feathers out right away, and yet I was permitted to take some. When I tried to pull one more, I couldn't. I had been given my quota so I gave thanks, then I picked up the hawk and removed it from the road. I have some of those feathers on my walking stick, and some in the vehicle that I drive. I also gave great thanks because that was affirmation for me with regards to my father's spirit.

When I got to work, I was fine. I felt a real sense of peace because I knew my father left when he was ready and I had seen and felt the spirit leave. My mother was very nervous about being alone after my father passed away, so Vivian agreed to stay with her for a few days. At my parents' home, my father's spirit came to visit Vivian and my mother for the first couple of nights. Vivian told me that he looked just as he had when he had first married my mother. Apparently, my father stood in the doorway and watched my mother sleep, seeming quite pleased that she was not alone. Vivian watched him for a bit to see if he was going to do anything, and then rolled over and went back to sleep.

From time to time, I still sense my father's spirit guiding me. I truly believe that there is nothing in the spirit world that can hurt you. I believe that we are surrounded by unconditional love, wisdom, and knowledge at all times and those in the spirit world do not infringe on this beautiful gift of freedom of choice while we are learning here on earth. They can, however, give you subtle information or do subtle things that might make you look twice at something or stop you from doing something by helping you to reconsider the act.

RJ and I were growing further apart. I wasn't interested in most of the television programs he would watch, and vice versa. Consequently there was a television in the living room, where he would sit and flip through his channels merrily, and I would watch whatever I wanted to on the other television in the bedroom. He'd be drinking beer in the living room and I'd be in bed. By the time he decided to go to bed, I was already going to sleep. I wasn't interested in being kept up, since I had to work the next day. I had learned to value and honor myself, to love myself physically and say:

"No. I merit better than this. I'm not just a machine. I'm not just something for you to use whenever you want. It's time to start owning up to my truth and loving myself enough to be able to speak my truth and say no. This is not going to take place."

So, sexually, I told RJ I wasn't interested, and because of this we were in conflict all the time. Also, we were still dealing with lawyers over the house and he was supposed to be paying the bills. If a bill came in, or if he was harassed by a bill collector, he would complain to me, so there was never any reprieve. After the bill payments, any extra money was always spent on him, the kids, or was put aside for us to go out with.

The big night out was the bingo parlor.

We tried marriage counseling with Brenda, which was when I first met her, but after three months RJ decided he didn't want to go anymore. I continued to see her alone.

A year before we actually went our separate ways, I said to him: "This can't keep on. I'm not happy, you're not happy." And he would always reply, "Just tell me you want me to leave and I'll go. Just tell me."

By then, he was the only male figure my grandson Tommy really knew. RJ would go on splurges of doting on Tommy. Therefore, it wasn't so easy to leave him.

I finally told myself, "Okay. No more rose-colored glasses. It doesn't matter how much I care for him." I had learned that you can love somebody but disapprove of their behavior or dislike it intensely.

Then one day, I came home from work only to be served with an eviction notice. The house was being repossessed for failure to pay taxes.

I looked at RJ and demanded, "Where is this coming from? We paid our taxes. We made arrangements last year, and prior to that. We went to a lawyer and agreed to pay the taxes at fifty dollars a month."

We were supposed to have received warnings: *Either pay, or else. You have sixty days to comply . . .*

"I never saw those letters," I said.

"They never came," he told me.

This was too much for Vivian, who turned around and said, "I'm tired of you pulling this on Mom," and then marched over to RJ's stash of stuff and pulled the letter out that he had received months before. It was addressed to both of us, asking if we intended to comply and pay our taxes. Here he was, telling me point blank that he had never gotten it. Now, we had thirty days to leave the house.

"You know, RJ, this is it. *This is it.*"

From 1995 to 2001 I fought for that house, fought RJ's drinking habits, fought his resentment, his bitterness, and his jealousies. My mind started going through everything, and I thought, "No. I can't do this."

"RJ, I've got to tell you, we've lost this home, and I am not repeating this. We've got thirty days to get the hell out of here. Where are we supposed to go after a big house like this?"

"You're telling me to get out then? You're telling me to get out then?" RJ repeated.

"Do what you want to do, but I'm not going back to this kind of life."

RJ's son, Michael, lived in Carleton Place but was heading back to Ottawa permanently. Vivian had spoken to Michael, as had I, to make sure that his one-bedroom apartment, which was cheap to rent, would be kept for his father. I wanted RJ's kids to know that there were no prejudices on my part. Vivian and I moved all of RJ's stuff in.

Two or three days prior to the eviction, I had found out that Rachel and her husband had sold everything and were moving to China for a year to teach. They left at the beginning of December, so I had been trying to adjust to their departure. Vivian, Tommy, and I now had no place to live, so we moved into a motel. Twenty-four hours later, we got an emergency call at four o'clock in the morning, from China. Rachel and her husband had been caught in a scam. When they had arrived, there were no jobs waiting for them. They were stranded with my grandson, André, with no money to get back. They had no place to live or sleep and they were absolutely terrified. Their safe return took priority, so Vivian and I scrambled to raise funds to bail them out and get them home. In the meantime, we had to put them up at a motel, which cost an astronomical amount of money. I borrowed money from friends, even my stepson helped, and three days later Rachel and family were back home.

I found myself living in a motel room with my daughter Rachel, her husband, their son, and their big black lab, my two poodles, my daughter Vivian, and her son Tommy. It took us two weeks to find a place. Every day we'd check *The Citizen* newspaper until we found an old farmhouse in Stittsville. It was to be our new home. I was back with my girls once more. A new chapter of our lives had begun.

It took me a long time to stop and look at the lessons, but it was what I chose to experience. As a consequence, I have grown emotionally, spiritually, and ethereally. One of the things that took me a long time to do was take off those rose-colored glasses. Near the end of my second marriage, I was beginning to like myself more, to appreciate myself more and honor myself, but I was still refusing to look at the true picture. For instance, I gave RJ the responsibility of handling all the finances even though I knew that things weren't being done the way they were supposed to. I chose to keep a blind eye to it. Finally, it reached a point where I had to deal with the reality, even though I didn't want to go through a period of learning from some of these unpleasant moments that I had helped to create. As I said to my Creator:

"You know you need to hit me with a sledgehammer, because I'm going to ignore the lessons until then."

The experience reinforced the idea that I needed to look closely at the situations I had lived through. By doing that, I had a stronger hold on my truth so that I could continue to evolve and grow. I finally could love myself unconditionally because I had forgiven myself. I can honestly say that I have no animosity or hatred towards any role that was played in my life journey, by myself or anyone else.

What I was slower to do was acknowledge that I had willingly put on rose-colored glasses so I wouldn't have to deal with any of the truth in my relationship with RJ. And after I faced all those truths within myself, I found I grew stronger, as did that sense of loving myself unconditionally. I took off the rose-colored glasses and decided to stop running from all these truths. Then all I wanted to do was evolve and continue to grow so my abilities could strengthen and so I could have a greater impact when helping people in their own learning process.

Letting go of that marriage was a very painful process because I had spent twenty years with RJ, so any feelings and longings we shared were not going to go away overnight. It was a challenge for me to acknowledge that I couldn't hold him responsible, a challenge to turn around and say:

"I chose to suffer the consequences of this situation so that these lessons would stay with me. And I chose the moment when I would look at those truths and deal with them."

I learned to honor myself by walking away from my first husband Ivan, accepting that it was a learning experience, and forgiving myself for some of the journeys I took. After facing that truth, and gathering the wisdom and gifts that came with it, I can now share it with all those who cross my path. With RJ, I honored myself by pulling out of the screenplay life that stunted my growth and diminished who I was. By doing so, I was also honoring him.

When you are ready to look at the picture, learn the lessons from your experiences, and forgive yourself, there is no room for anger and animosity because you grow beyond it. You can put yourself in a space and time that nourish you as a whole.

I feel a sense of peace, now that the battle is over, but I move slowly because I don't want to be pushed into something for which I'm not ready. I'm at an age where I want the lessons to come a little more gently. I was never able to relax for a good many years simply because I was on such a roller coaster ride in my private life. Now, I implement things like a walk when I need it. Or, I'll allow myself the luxury of a diversion. It was something I never seemed to be able to do before. I lived in a world of "demand, demand, demand" and made myself the sole designated fixer-upper for the planet. That was also part of my preconditioning because I wanted to make right all the things that were wrong. Now that I've opened the doorway and acknowledged the lessons, forgiven myself, and experienced unconditional love, I'm the one in control now — not all the yesterdays.

I've walked a lot of roads. I got caught up in the fear. But I reached a point where I really began to look at the positives from those episodes in my life, and that is the first step towards creating a connection with the ethereal and the Creator. Take a good look at all of those yesterdays. Then, you can see how to change your life for a better tomorrow.

EXERCISE:

How often and in what ways do you honor yourself? Creating a serenity room is a start, but how do you honor yourself in your daily life? Take some time to sit down with your journal and consider all the ways that you honor your physical, emotional, and spiritual self. Remember, the simple things count as well. When you have your list, ask yourself how often these come into play. It is important to honor yourself during the calmer times in life, but even more important to honor yourself when you are going through times of stress. It is during those times when we often forget the importance of looking after ourselves. If you are one of those individuals who often forgets to honor yourself, then take that list you've written and place it somewhere visible as a reminder. Make it colorful, or obvious enough so that it won't get lost in the shuffle of day-to-day life.

SESSION SIX

Visions

My visions occur in seven steps. Here are three examples of seven-step visions I have personally recorded.

August 4, 1998

1. I see a calm lake and I am watching people cooking, walking, chatting, laughing. . . . I am sitting on my heels across from Sitting Bull. There is a fire between us. White Eagle Head is dancing and chanting while shaking his rattle to the left of us. I see a very tall totem pole, at the top of which I know sits the eagle. The pole stands so high, it goes beyond the clouds, yet I can feel the eagle watching over everyone.

2. I ask Sitting Bull: "Will the people be saved? How will we know this safety?" Sitting Bull answers with a vision. Daylight turns to nighttime, I see shooting stars in the sky. It is beautiful to see, the heavens are alive and to the far northern distance I can see the lights of many colors dancing in the sky. I smile for my heart is filled with love and wonderment.

3. I ask: "How can I help? What am I to do?" I can see myself walking, giving small pouches to men, women, and children. I have no fear, for whatever direction I turn to there are four distinct figures who surround me and walk with me.

4. "Will I be able to persuade my family to come with me on my journey?" Sitting Bull replies: "All but one will give you problems, but eventually all will follow."

5. "What tools will I have to accomplish this quest?" Sitting Bull scratches a hole in the earth. I see him dropping some seeds and covering them. I notice a large tree sprout, and water trickling from its base. Then Sitting Bull hands me a blanket, a turtle rattle, and a large pouch that holds many seeds, followed by a second large pouch that holds many smaller pouches that I am to give to the people. As Sitting Bull gives me these objects, I see a very tall bear behind him, smiling.

6. "Sitting Bull, will you always be there to guide me?" He brings his fist to his heart and as he brings his fist back a bright object is in his hand, which he places on my chest over my heart, and smiles. Then he points to White Eagle Head, the sun dancer, and smiles and nods. I am overcome with feelings of love, joy, and peace.

7. Sitting Bull then places his left hand on my head, lifts a rattle with his right hand, and begins singing and

chanting over me. I feel the gentle spray of water on my
face. I see his smiling eyes as the vision slowly fades away.

In native teachings, the Eagle symbolizes Spirit; the ability to live in the spirit realm yet remain grounded. The Turtle represents Mother Earth; grounding, the creative source within, and developing ideas before bringing them to light.

December 27, 1998

1. Snow-capped mountains in the background. . . . Running stream with a rainbow over it. . . . Silver fish that sparkle like gems diving through the rainbow back into the stream.

2. I see myself squatting on my heels with Sitting Bull sitting across from me in front of an open animal skin.

3. I notice White Eagle Head dancing and chanting, shaking his turtle rattle, while Walking Buffalo Head comes forward shaking his long tube with three feathers at each end. I see a ceremonial mask smiling.

4. Two Feathers is walking clockwise around Sitting Bull and myself, I am to his left sitting on my heels. From a clay bowl she is sprinkling us with water while chanting.

5. Sitting Bull reaches over and ties three ermine tails to my hair next to the three feathers that already seem to be attached there, then wraps me in a large white fur skin.

6. I look up and see seven bears: three behind me and three behind Sitting Bull — two black, two brown, two grizzly. For some reason at this point I seem to be across from him with the skin between us. On the side where the stream is, a large polar bear is standing.

7. There is a large oak behind Sitting Bull. On the stream side on a low branch sits an eagle, on the right side on a low branch sits a raven. From a pouch at their waist Walking Buffalo Head and White Eagle Head begin to throw some kind of dust that shimmers and glows in the air towards the tree. The oak transforms into a tall shimmering being, so tall that I cannot see his face. I am told he is Manitou. I notice a canoe with a man in it paddling towards us on the stream. The canoe is loaded with skins. Sitting Bull opens my left hand and puts three branches in it: white pine, sycamore, and ash. He smiles then disappears as the vision fades.

The Bear represents Introspection; attuning the self with the inner energies and understanding that the answers all lie within the spirit. To dream of future goals allows them to become concrete realities. The Raven symbolizes Magic, or the Void; Raven brings a change of consciousness.

January 31, 1999

1. I am squatting on my heels across from an Elder, whom I believe to be Sitting Bull. There is a fire burning between us. I notice a large tree behind him transforming into a large eagle.

2. I look to my left and see mountains that are snow-capped in the distance. I see the large white teepee near the shore of a running stream. A large white buffalo with two young calves stands grazing near the tent.

3. Two Feathers is standing close to my right and to the far right I see a fire circle, hollow in the center and burning brightly with warriors dancing around it.

4. Off to the right of the fire circle are two hills. I notice White Eagle Head is holding a white pine shaft in his hands. He is digging at the base of these hills with the staff. Water starts slowly trickling out of the ground towards the dancing warriors.

5. Sitting Bull slowly unfolds and opens a polar bear rug in front of him. On the rug sit three pipes: one is long with feathers, one is medium length, and one is short. There are also a pair of moccasins, a water holder, and a pouch with rice on this rug.

6. Sitting Bull reaches over to me and puts the rice pouch on one shoulder, the water holder on the other shoulder. He lights the pipes one at a time, chants a prayer, and blows smoke on the moccasins from each pipe, then returns the pipes to the polar bear skin.

7. Sitting Bull reaches over and gently puts the moccasins on my feet and motions me to stand. I start walking as he

points to the White Buffalo, then he slowly fades away.

The Buffalo represents Abundance and Prayer; giving thanks and praise for gifts in life, embracing prayer and honoring the pathways of others. In August of 2000, I was adopted by Bert Larocque, Micmac White Buffalo clan.

EXERCISE:

A great many of my clients ask me if I meditate on a regular basis. My standard answer is, "No, not in the yoga sense of meditation." And it is with honor that I'm saying this, not taking away from any traditional teachings. My personal interpretation of meditation is drifting, which translates to a moment of time (as we know it in this world) where I allow my mind, body, and spirit to become one and just float in "no-time." The closest relation to drifting is daydreaming, or the state just before we fall asleep. I don't try to control the thoughts or feelings that take place. In complete trust, should anything occur while I am drifting that is of paramount importance to acknowledge, I will have total recall and will take note of it when I return from the beautiful, restful journey. Then I ask for guidance as to its interpretation or to bring forth those who can assist me in recognizing the message. When you daydream and allow yourself to drift, you've surrendered yourself to the world that is beyond this earth. Sit down somewhere quiet and let yourself slide into that "no-time" zone. Look out a window and let your mind, body, and spirit go into that state of semi-consciousness and let whatever transpires come with ease. Allow yourself to interact with the images with ease because this isn't the time to question, analyze, or discern the message. Rather, it is a time of serenity, relaxation, and receiving. Once you come back from drifting, then write down the messages received (with no prejudice) in your journal. Let the insights come in time.

She Who Hears from the Winds

My first exposure to the native community came after my experience with the Mohawk ceremonial mask. I had met a couple who were non-native, who followed many native traditions. They called me up and asked if I wanted to join them at a spiritual gathering weekend in Maniwaki. Maniwaki ("Land of Mary" in Algonquin) is a city in Quebec, and just south of the city is the *Réserve de la Rivière Désert*, or the Kitigan Zibi Reserve. I didn't really know much about the weekend, or what it entailed, but once they explained it to me, I was excited.

So off we went. That was the weekend I met elder William Commanda, keeper of sacred belts: The Jay Treaty Belt, The Seven Fires Prophecy Belt, and The Peace Treaty Belt of 1701. That's also where I met Grayhawk, a Cherokee elder and teacher. And that's where my journey began.

Grayhawk works with street youth and the school system, among other things. Like my own, his teaching philosophy focuses on finding and acknowledging your truth center, and forgiving yourself. When he teaches, along with William Commanda and another man I have come to learn a great deal from, Sequoya Trueblood, it's always without judgment or prejudice. This has been such a great asset for me. I would have to say the last ten years with these people have been the greatest teaching and learning times of my life.

During the weekend in Maniwaki, various activities were organized, including male and female sweat lodges, vision quests, and spiritual teachings. After all these experiences, along with watching the ceremonies, I had such a sense of completion. That opened the door for me and I realized why I always felt like a misfit when it came to structured religion. It was always fear and negativity I was breathing in, rather than the true essence of the Creator and the unconditional love for which it stood. When I listened to the philosophies behind native spirituality, I had a real sense of going one step higher in my understanding. It was a *knowing.* I've been going back annually to the spiritual gathering in Maniwaki ever since.

Because the native community is very active in dealing with spirituality and the spirit world, and they connect so readily with life and the planet that we live on, there is always a sense of learning, teaching, prayer, and giving thanks. I was so comfortable with those philosophies, it seemed very natural for me to fit in to their way of life. I found that elders and teachers were naturally crossing my path and I was able to share some of my visions with them and gain a greater understanding of what those visions represented. To have my visions translated and affirmed, with total acceptance, was wonderful.

By the time I met Brenda and started working with her, I had already met a couple of great teachers. One of them was Willaru, from Peru. I had had the opportunity to attend some of his teachings and meet him personally before he went back home. Willaru takes people on excursions to some of the most sacred Peruvian sites. Sequoya Trueblood, another teacher in my life, is part Cheyenne and works with those in the prison system. By the time these teachers have finished their sessions, you actually have a heightened sense of awareness and knowing. Their teachings are all about self-growth, self-awareness, forgiveness, release, and connecting with a higher ethereal level. You learn about acceptance of others, whether you agree or disagree with their choices.

I am always in contact with Grayhawk. If I go on a vision quest, I'll call Grayhawk to get his perspective. I'll do the same thing with Sequoya. Unfortunately, I can only see Willaru once or twice a year when he comes to this part of the world. In life, we are both teachers and students. Finding teachers that support your own personal journey is not only beneficial from an educational standpoint, but it creates a support network for you while you move forward with your growth.

One thing Grayhawk speaks of is the power of the circle. His poem, "Singing Dreams," dedicated to Grandfather Commanda, talks of people as they come together in the circle of life.

The sky is round, and I have heard that the earth is like a ball, and so are the stars. The wind in its greatest power, whirls. Birds make their nests in Circles, for theirs is the same religion as ours. The sun comes forth and goes down again in a Circle. The moon does the same, and both are round. Even the seasons form a great Circle in their changing, and always come back again to where they were. The life of a person is a Circle from childhood to childhood, and so it is in everything where power moves.

Everybody's equal in the circle. Doesn't matter if you're a judge, a street gang leader, a politician, or a cop, everyone has equal status and that's the beginning of the healing and learning. We can begin to understand each other and transform our world. We are all children and we are all growing and learning. When we are in a circle, we can do so together. Grayhawk speaks of the Medicine Wheel, and how everything has its place in the wheel of life. This wheel is "a map of knowledge, showing what we need in order to be in harmony with ourselves, and other people in this world." If you find yourself in conflict within your family, or within a group, bringing everyone together in a circle to discuss issues openly can be very effective.

In August of 2000, I was honored by being adopted into the White Buffalo clan by Bert Larocque. Bert is part of the Micmac tribe, and lives in Nova Scotia. His wife, Jeorgina, is an elder and a medicine woman. I had met them through some mutual friends at a spiritual gathering at Grandfather William Commanda's in Maniwaki. Through many conversations over the last couple of years, I had grown to such a level of comfort with the community that I felt it was where I truly belonged. That's when the opportunity arose for me to be adopted by Bert.

A full ceremony occurred, with Grandmother Jeorgina officiating the event. I have some friends who live in a beautiful home by a babbling creek. The ceremony was held there with native and non-native friends and family. Designs representing north, south, east, and west were made on the ground with special seeds, native prayers were spoken, and a sacred fire was lit. During the ceremony, my body was anointed with oils and grease as symbols were drawn on my skin. Then I provided an offering to my new father for adopting me, as well as gifting Grandmother Jeorgina with tobacco.

The name given to me was Windsong. It originally came from one of my visions years prior to the ceremony. That particular vision was one of the first ones that I had recorded. I was told in this vision that I would be known as "she who hears from the winds," and that an elder would give me the name. Then, several months after that vision, I met Grandfather William Commanda. He was the one who told me the name in the Algonquin language.

As I mentioned, I would often call upon Grayhawk or Sequoya when looking for their interpretation of one of my visions. I also had some other interesting experiences when it came to my gifts and my native friends. A couple of years ago, I went to a native community to visit with a friend of mine who is the Grand Chief of her community. I wanted to see everything on the reservation. She had family members who were buried in a nearby graveyard, so I suggested we go and visit. Five of us got in a car to go.

I've always been fascinated with graveyards, even at a very early age. I always acknowledged the people inside. It would always upset me to see a desecrated graveyard. To me it's the highest form of disrespect to those who have, in one way or another, touched people's lives. By desecrating the stones, the message left is that the lives of these people were useless, the spirit world is useless, and so the Creator is useless. Unconditional love is useless. Any lessons these people gave meant nothing. That was how I translated it, and to this day, I still feel that way. So when I get the opportunity to visit a graveyard, I will go in order to say thank you to those who once walked this earth.

As we were driving down the lane towards the reservation's graveyard, I yelled at the driver: "Watch out! You're going to hit the man!"

The driver slammed on the brakes.

"What man?"

"Oh," I said, realizing the situation. "That's okay. Just pull off to the side. I now know what I'm seeing."

We got out of the vehicle, and they watched me.

"His name's Jerome," I said.

Jerome stood only about five-foot-ten. He was slight in build. He was wearing old jeans and an old checked shirt buttoned right to the neck. His salt and pepper hair was unkempt. He was native, but he had light hazel eyes and looked very intense. His face was weather-worn as were his hands, suggesting that he had done a lot of work in his lifetime.

The chief looked at me and said, "Jerome? I don't remember any native ever called Jerome, at least not in this community."

"Well," I said, "He tells me his name is Jerome. You have a responsibility. We're going to walk through this graveyard until we find a gravestone with Jerome's name on it. His wife's name is on it. Her date of birth is on it, but she hasn't passed away yet. She's very ill, she's alone, and she's going to die in agony. It's your responsibility to find her, wherever she is, and make sure she's not alone in her final hours."

"What?" the chief said, surprised.

I said, "I'm telling you. We've got to find this grave marking first. Start walking!"

We went row upon row, looking at the gravestones. I continued watching Jerome, who just stood there, silently.

"I'm doing it," I said to him.

Finally, after twenty minutes of searching, I said, "Okay, Jerome, you want us to find this grave marking. You had better show me. What are you standing there for? Bring us right to it."

No sooner did I say that when all of a sudden one of the people turned around and said, "I found it!"

This individual had started in the far corner of the graveyard. So we went over, and sure enough, the grave was marked with Jerome's full name, date of birth, and death, and the first name of his wife, her date of birth, but not her day of passing.

So the chief said to me, "I don't think the woman is from this community. I haven't heard of her."

So I looked up. Jerome was still standing there. I heard him saying, "*Well not right on the reservation, but she's in this area.*"

I said, "Not on the reservation but in this area."

"Are you hearing anything else?" she asked.

All of a sudden Jerome was gone.

"He's gone," I told her, "But you've got a job. You'd better find her."

I had to head back the next day, but I called every day after I returned.

"Did you find her?"

Jerome was plaguing me mentally day and night. It was six days later when the chief called me.

"Judy . . . I found her. She's very ill. I had her brought to the hospital. I'm with her. I'll be in every day and I'll see that she goes into a proper facility to be cared for."

She was in a lot of pain, this older woman in her eighties. She was taken to a nursing home once she had been released from the hospital. She lived there for about two months, and died peacefully in her sleep.

It turned out that Jerome was native, but not full-blooded. He was half-French, half-native and his wife was not native. That's why she had not been on the reservation.

I had another interesting experience when I went to visit Grayhawk in Massachusetts. When I was in my early thirties, I used to do a lot of acrylic oil paintings, and I even sold a few of them. At one point, while at a friend's home, I was painting on black velvet and I wasn't sure what I was going to paint. My colors were all set up, and as I started painting, I went into a sort of trance. I painted for about six hours. The friend who I was staying with knew that I would often drift, so she did not interfere. In a way, I was fortunate that it took place there. When I came out of the trance, I looked at the painting. I had painted an old stone house, similar to a little cottage. It was set in a wood clearing. The interesting part was that I had signed it "Sarah of Salem."

When the people I was staying with saw the picture, they

were fascinated. They asked me if I would gift them the picture. I agreed, and left the picture with them. But that memory stayed with me for years, and for some reason I had chosen not to question why I had signed it "Sarah of Salem." On another note, all my life I have had a fascination with being under the water but I had a tremendous fear of being on top of it. I have also had an obsessive fear of fire and I never ventured to find out why.

About a year ago, I had an opportunity to stay with Grayhawk and his wife Linda in their home in the United States. The second day that I was there, Linda asked me if there was any place that I'd like to go and visit.

She said, "You always seem to express an interest in history, so how would you like to go to Salem to visit some of the historical sites there?"

I jumped at the opportunity. We planned to spend a full day there, just the two of us. When we reached Salem, the first couple of hours were great. We were just hob-nobbing here and there, looking at some of the small shops. Eventually, we entered one of the wax museums. The museum focused on the famous witch trials that had occurred in Salem in 1692.

Beside each wax figure was a plaque explaining the identity of the individual, the role they had played during the trials, how the situation began, and how it escalated into total madness. I went from plaque to plaque and figure to figure, taking my time. At one point, I did a left-hand turn to go to the next plaque, and I froze. I was overcome with such intense fear, sadness, and repulsion. It absolutely consumed me.

"What's the matter, Judy? What's going on?" Linda asked.

I explained what I was feeling, and what was happening.

"Do you want to leave? You're as white as a ghost."

"No," I said. "I want to make myself go over there and find out why I reacted this way."

I crossed the room to where a wax figure was on display. It represented a gentleman who had been crushed to death. He had eventually been branded as a witch, but prior to his death he had exposed a great many of the victims who had been executed. He had even turned in his own wife, whose name was Sarah.

After reading it, the sense of total horror, fear, and repulsion lifted to some degree, but I still felt it. I continued my visit through the museum, and at the end of the display was a list of names of the victims. There were about sixteen Sarah's listed there. Immediately, I had a vision of the house that I had painted twenty years earlier. As it flashed in my mind, I had a real sense of having been in Salem at that period of time. I decided that I had seen enough and I wanted to get out of there. We spent another half an hour just walking around as I gathered my wits and dismissed what had transpired. Then, I felt a tremendous pull to want to walk in the graveyard. Walking amid the old tombstones, I felt a real sense of kinship. By the time the day had ended, and we had returned to Linda and Grayhawk's home, I was bubbling with thoughts while trying to explain all my feelings to Grayhawk. I usually wake up at least once a night. That night, I slept soundly.

୫ଛ

On my wall is a painting of a native man with weathered skin and longish, grayish salt and pepper hair. He's wearing jeans with a belt, a light blue denim shirt, and cowboy boots. He has a leather pouch around his neck, and his hands are open. Behind him is a circle. Inside the circle is a white buffalo. At the four compass points of north, south, east, and west are stick dolls with square heads, little slit eyes, and four long slit arms each.

About four months before I even thought, on a conscious level, about leaving my husband RJ, the native man in the painting woke me up in the middle of the night. The painting did not exist at this point, yet I had dreamt that he was standing exactly the way he's now standing, staring at me with a hint of a smile. I yelled at him: "No!" Then I woke up. He plagued me for a day or two because my dream had been so vivid. A week or so before my husband and I split up, I dreamt of him again. He wore the same clothing and stood in the same stance. Again, I woke from the sound of my own voice yelling: "I told you, no!"

Shortly after RJ and I separated, I dreamt of the native man again. But this time, instead of yelling, I woke up exhausted because I spent the entire dream running away from him. At this point, he was really plaguing me, popping into my mind at different times during the day. I was really getting annoyed. I kept saying, "I'm not ready to deal with this. I don't want to know." So I kept pushing him back.

In March of 2002, he resurfaced in my dream. This time, however, I stood and faced him. Part of me was defiant, telling him I was not running anywhere, and another part of me wanted to know what he wanted from me. When I woke up, he continued to plague me. I knew he had a message, but I just wasn't ready to hear it. I thought, "I can't keep doing this, but my plates are full. I don't want to go there at this time." He wouldn't let me go. He just kept popping in my head.

So I thought of a woman I know who paints and also has gifts, and decided to ask her to create an oil painting of this man. I got in touch with her and gave her the general description. I didn't tell her about the buckle on his belt: a horseshoe made out of native turquoise. Nor did I tell her about the leather pouch around his neck.

"I don't know if I can paint this just from what you're telling me," she said.

"What I'd like you to do is to let yourself drift and see what you can do," I said.

"Well," she said, "we can always paint over the canvas if it doesn't end up being what you're looking for."

She called me up about three weeks later.

"I finished it. Come on over and take a look."

Right afterwards, I felt that sense of denial again, unprepared to deal with the situation, so I didn't go. About three months went by before she called me up again.

"Judy, you've got to do something. I don't know what it is about this person that is in the painting. I don't even know if I've got the right person, but I've got to tell you, I've locked it in the cupboard, I've put it in every room, I've had it face the wall. . . . It won't let me sleep."

So I finally conceded and thought, "All right. I'm going to go down and have a look."

I went to her home, and the minute I saw the picture, I knew she had captured him, even adding all the details that I had never mentioned to her. What intrigued me was the background. The white buffalo was appropriate, considering I had been adopted by that particular clan. The little stick dolls representing the four directions also had meaning. I had been gifted dolls like this before. The first one came in the mail from a friend, before I left RJ, and just before I went to see the picture, another woman that I know who collects different things gifted me with a little box with one of those dolls painted on the lid. Remember, there's no such thing as coincidence. I made no comment to my artist friend about either of these incidents. I thanked her for the painting, and took it home.

I was in the midst of getting my new place upgraded and painted. I took the canvas, and put it in my serenity room, facing the wall.

"You're going to stay right there. Don't bother me," I told him, "That's where you stay."

I kept him in there for about two weeks. But I kept having this sense of urgency.

"This is not where I belong, this is not where I belong."

So a couple of weeks later I said, "Okay, I'm going to make a compromise. I'll place you in a frame behind glass for protection."

I didn't want to invest in an expensive frame so I called up a friend of mine who had an old frame for me. The frame had a little crack in the lower right corner of the glass. I took the canvas out of the serenity room, and put it in the frame. In the broken corner, I put some sage, and I don't know why, but I was compelled to put a pink rose there also. Then, I mounted it in the bedroom. For the first month in my new home, I woke up a dozen times with the sense of the native man's physical presence being in the bedroom. I haven't yet determined what his message is, or opened myself to it. I'm not completely ready yet, but I know this home suits him.

Sometimes, we may not understand what the ethereal is telling us, or we may not be ready to hear their messages. Yet, that does not mean the messages are not there to be heard. The "winds" are full of wisdom. It's up to us to listen.

EXERCISE:

After I drift and before I work, I smudge myself with sage. I liken this native practice to incense used in structured religion or in Eastern beliefs. To me, it is a tool and an acknowledgement: another way to honor myself, all that is, and call upon the Creator to assist me at all levels. It is also a way to give thanks for all I have and all that I am today. Dried sage can be found in most new age stores. Light the end of one leaf, let it burn for a moment before blowing out the flame. Then, allow the ember to burn, creating a sweet smoke. Imagine you are bathing yourself in the smoke, letting it cleanse your aura.

Final Thoughts

I went through a lot of challenges with my gifts, and I see my daughters Vivian and Rachel undergoing some of those same trials. I can remember a time when I wouldn't acknowledge my gifts. I had enough on my plate. There were days, however, when the ethereal would not be ignored. I would put a plant in the corner, turn around, and the plant would be across the room. Or I'd say, "I *swore* I put my purse in the middle of the table. How come it's in the middle of the couch?"

The entities would do subtle things to insist that I paid attention. You do feel like you're going crazy for a period of time when some of this is happening. When you grow up in an atmosphere where you are constantly being put down and told that you are not bright, or that there's something wrong with you mentally, it only makes you question your sanity more. When I was growing up, I quit sharing because I got tired of hearing that there was something wrong with me.

There are always entities around. My oldest grandson is going through a phase now where he's seeing a black dog. Vivian saw a black cat when she was a teenager, even though we never had a black cat. She'd see it following her down the hall. It would flip her out. Even as a kid, Vivian would know or sense that there were things around. Most of my family lived with this ability for awhile, even if they didn't acknowledge it.

I know one of my brothers had gifts but he buried himself into drugs. My older sister has admitted to me on several occasions that she sees and hears spirits. My younger sister is very attuned. She feels things and knows that they're there, but it still frightens her. One of my mother's sisters was attuned to the ethereal world and would give readings. My mother always had these gifts, but would never talk about them. As a child, I was told that it was just my imagination or it was "just a dream, forget about it." Even today, parents often dismiss children. Children are often giving you a lot of messages that you may not be listening to.

Every time I was pregnant, I knew what I was carrying and if I would lose it, before it was confirmed medically that I was pregnant. I would dream of the child. If I saw the child's face, I knew the child would survive. If I didn't see the child's face, I knew I was going to lose that child. I carried three males that I lost, and the others were female. I was totally connected with the children that I carried.

Having gifts was tough when my girls were teenagers. I knew if Vivian had skipped school, for example. Sometimes I would call them on it, but for the most part I let my girls do what normal teenagers do. I had a hard time simply because I was always afraid of something happening to them, or somebody taking advantage of them. Even though I couldn't use the gifts for myself, I was given the opportunity to know if there was something out of the ordinary that the kids were up to, and that was very difficult. That was the first time that I began to realize the importance of being able to walk and deal realistically in the world. I discovered the true meaning of freedom of choice, and I had no right to interfere with that. It was their choice to grow and learn in this world, and sometimes being in this world is a constant battle. Being a mother, I didn't want them to do or experience certain things, but that was their decision. It took me a number of years to realize that I didn't have the right to infringe.

The ethereal world and the Creator are always there as support, if you ask. Let's say I am getting ready to go to work and something occurs out of left field that creates undue stress. I know at that moment that I'm not yet at the point where I can objectively look at the whole picture. The stress is having its effect on me mentally and emotionally, and I realize that I have to be at work in half an hour. I know I'm not going to be able to give as much as I should be giving when I'm dealing with the client, so I now say to the Creator: "Please, take care of it for me."

I'll then walk into my office knowing I have six or seven people booked and confirmed, and I'm still not ready to deal with a client. But I trust that the Creator will come through for me. As I'm walking through the door, the phone rings and the receptionist picks it up: "Judy, you just had your first three clients cancel. They've been rebooked for another day." This enables me to compose myself in the free time, which benefits everyone. It is always taken care of — always.

Like many people, my schedule is full at work all day, and I'm tired afterwards. Sometimes, if I've got several other things to do, I can feel my anxiety level rising. When this happens, I say: "Make this go away."

Bang! Something inadvertently will happen to totally distract me so that I'm pulled away from that moment. It could be something as simple as the phone ringing, and it turns out to be a friend I haven't heard from in five years. While catching up, the whole scenario changes. Suddenly, I'm laughing and calm. By the time I get off the phone, half an hour or maybe an hour later, I'm in a totally different mood. So when it's time to continue with my long list of things to do, I have a healthy perspective. The anxiety, fear's cousin, is gone, and if all I manage to do is one more thing on the list, I'm now able to say, "That's fine, it wasn't meant to be." And I dismiss it. It's unimportant.

We all have a habit of holding other people responsible for everything that has taken place in our lives. You need to turn around and take full ownership of your experiences, and realize that there is nobody else responsible.

I will continue to work with the different clients that come to see me. My goal is to be in a position to really help people understand the three T's, so that they in turn have the ability to unconditionally love themselves. That love could then continue through the generations. By helping others to open up the doorway to the ethereal, they can strengthen their spiritual connection to the Creator, as they see the Creator. In my mind, if I can do this in some small way, perhaps in this world, in this dimension, the true sense of peace and unconditional love will grow. The caring, nurturing, and loving will then surpass all the fears that are out there that have been controlling generation after generation.

Once you start looking at your life experiences, and you acknowledge and accept your truth, then you find the positive in those negatives (the lessons learned) and you gift yourself with one of the greatest blessings — unconditional love. With each situation you heal, you now have the gift to share and to help heal those who may cross your path. Because of yesterday's experiences and all these roads I've journeyed, I have come to realize the true meaning of unconditional love. I have learned to love myself enough to accept that I've done all these things. I've forgiven myself and forgiven others. My hand is full when I offer it to somebody. You can pick and choose what you want from it. From my yesterdays, my experiences, pick the tool that you want to use so that you can learn, just for a moment, to love yourself unconditionally. That moment will breed another moment. Instead of creating a downward spiral, you can create an upward spiral. By using yesterday's lessons, you can move towards a positive tomorrow.

A friend of mine gifted me with a painting that I have called "The Forest of the Mist." Mist flows over a river, just before the edge of a thick wood. The mist represents the shadows, the smoke, and the mirrors of life. The forest represents all the things that are in life: the present reality. If you look closely, you can see the spirits and the guardians amid the trees, ready to reach out. Remember, they are always here for us. Even if you have difficulty picking them out at first, when the time is right, and you are ready, you will see them. You just need to look closely.

Recommended Readings

The following books helped me along my journey, and may be of great value to you as you continue on yours.

Bruce, Eve, M.D. *Shaman, M.D.: A Plastic Surgeon's Remarkable Journey into the World of Shapeshifting.* Vermont: Destiny Books, 2002.

Houston, Jean. *A Passion for the Possible: A Guide to Realizing Your True Potential.* New York: Harper SanFrancisco, 1998.

Kaltreider, Kurt. *American Indian Prophecies: Conversations with Chasing Deer.* California: Hay House, 1998.

Millman, Dan. *Way of the Peaceful Warrior.* New York: J.P. Tarcher, 1980.